buffalo soldiers: reVision

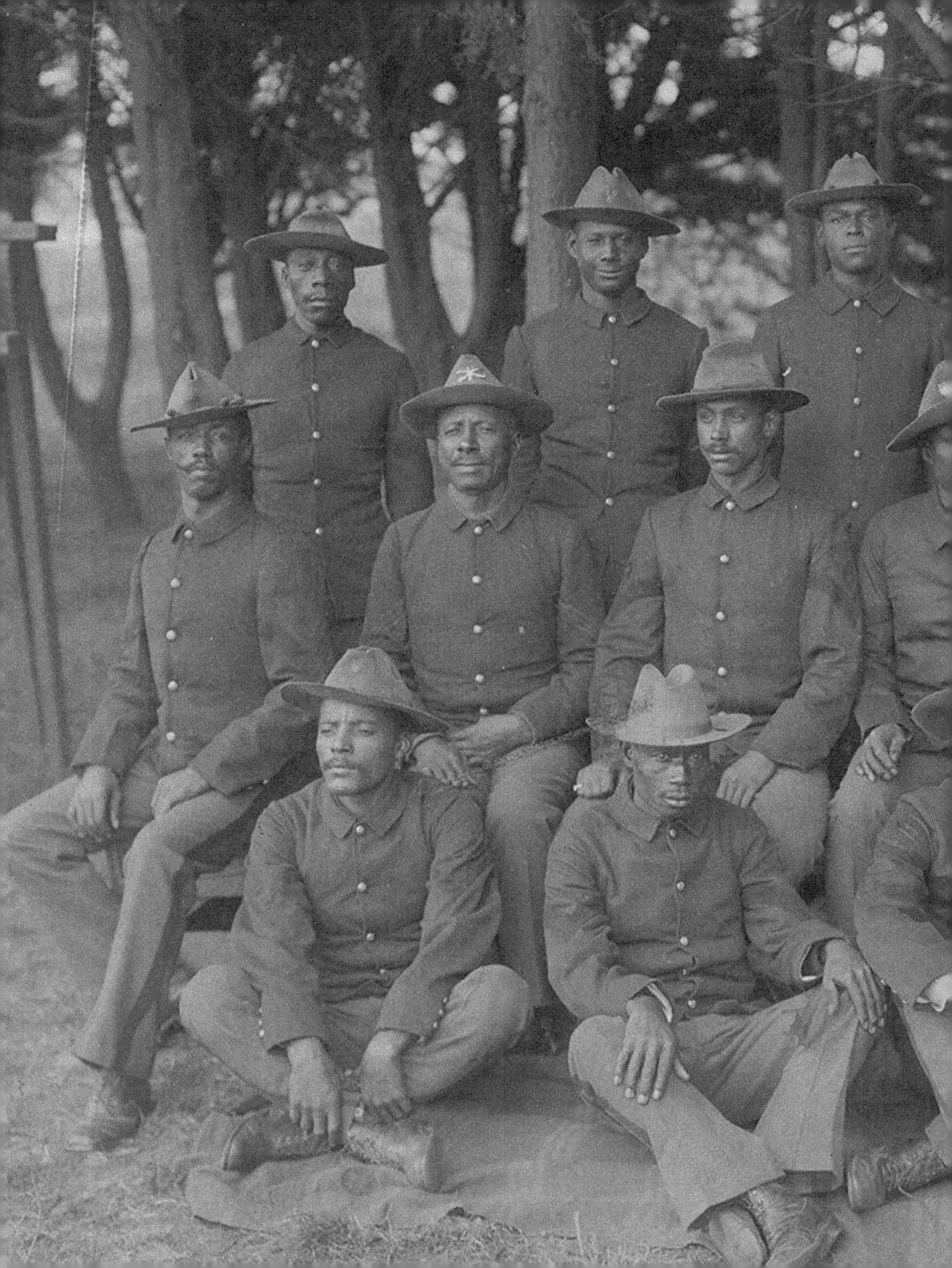

buffalo soldiers: reVision

Chip Thomas, editor

with contributions from
Esther Belin
Mahogany L. Browne
Eric Carpio
Rosie Carter
Gaia
André Leon Gray
Theodore A. Harris
Tom Judd

the fort garland museum & cultural center,
a community museum of history colorado

buffalo soldiers: reVision was organized by the Fort Garland Museum & Cultural Center, a Community Museum of History Colorado. Additional funding for the exhibition was provided by Arts In Society and the National Endowment for the Humanities.

The exhibition opened June 24, 2023, at the Fort Garland Museum & Cultural Center, Fort Garland, Colorado.

Chip Thomas, lead artist
with contributions from
Esther Belin
Mahogany L. Browne
Eric Carpio
Rosie Carter
Gaia
André Leon Gray
Theodore A. Harris
Tom Judd

Cover design by Chip Thomas
Text design and production by Patrick Barber
Set in Meno Text and Skolar Sans, with titles in Brother 1816 Printed and Special Elite.

Front cover: Dick "Buckskin" Charley and John Taylor, ca. 1888. DENVER PUBLIC LIBRARY

Inside cover: Bison skulls to be ground and used for fertilizer, fine bone china, carbon black pigment, and refining sugar. Michigan Carbon Works, Rougeville, Michigan, 1892. DETROIT PUBLIC LIBRARY

Frontispiece: Group photograph of 10th Cavalry soldiers, ca. 1900. Courtesy History Colorado—Denver, Colorado.

Back cover and pages 6–7: Eric J. Carpio, *White Shell Mountain (Blanca Peak),* photograph.

Pages 14–15: Photo illustration incorporating Eadweard Muybridge, *The Domes*, stereographic photograph of The Domes, Yosemite Valley, 1868. THE NEW YORK PUBLIC LIBRARY DIGITAL COLLECTIONS

Page 37: Detail of photo of Italian building with Buffalo Bill's Wild West poster displays wrapping around the first floor exterior, ca. 1906. OBJECT ID#302, BUFFALO BILL MUSEUM AND GRAVE, GOLDEN, COLORADO

Pages 52–53: Photo illustration incorporating photograph of Kitty Cloud, Euterpe Taylor, and others. DENVER PUBLIC LIBRARY

Page 100: 37 Star U.S. Flag flown at Fort Garland, 1869–1876. HISTORY COLORADO—DENVER, COLORADO

ISBN-13: 9798988013341

PRINTED AND DISTRIBUTED BY INGRAM PUBLISHING SERVICES

contents

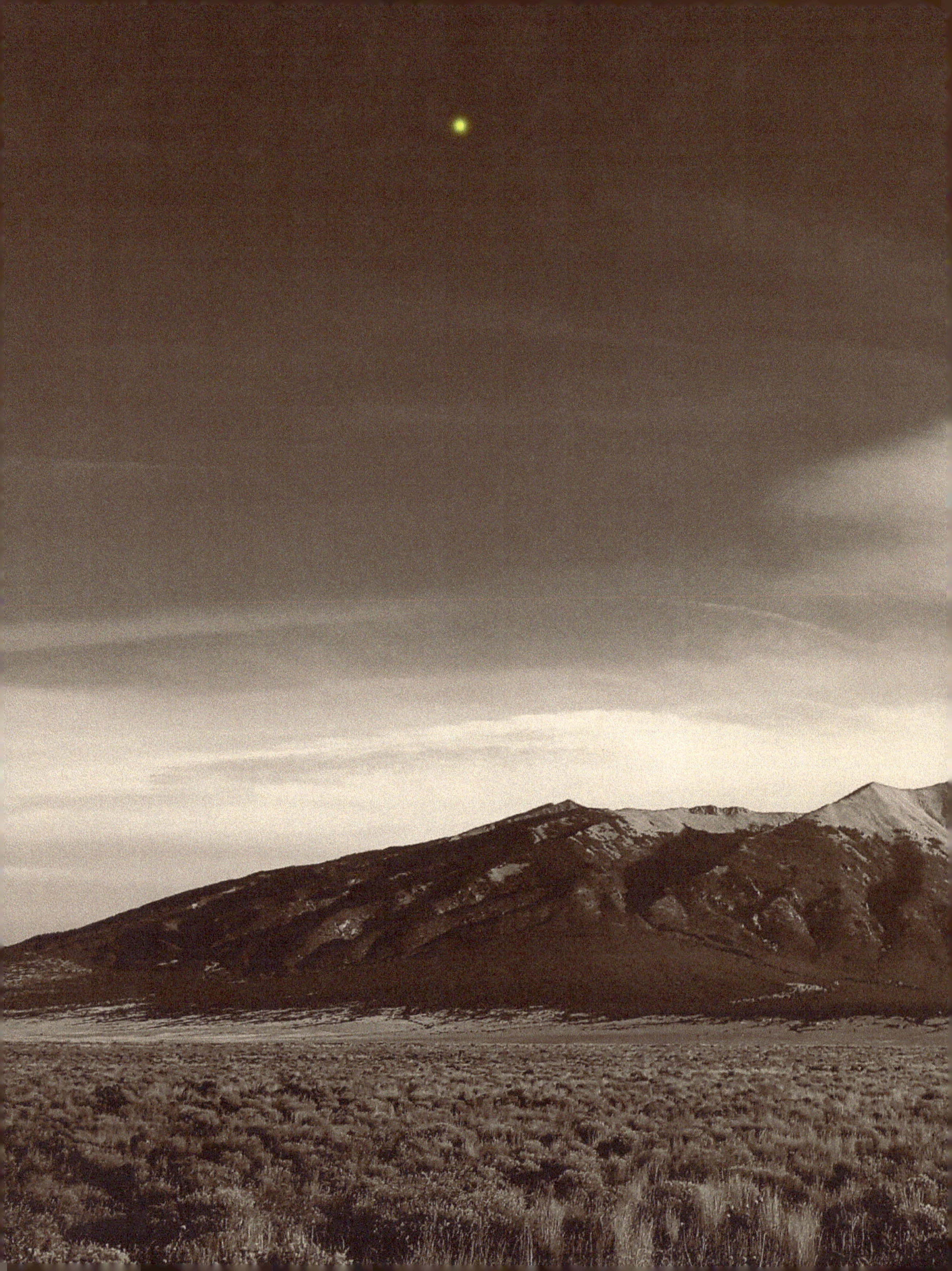

introduction

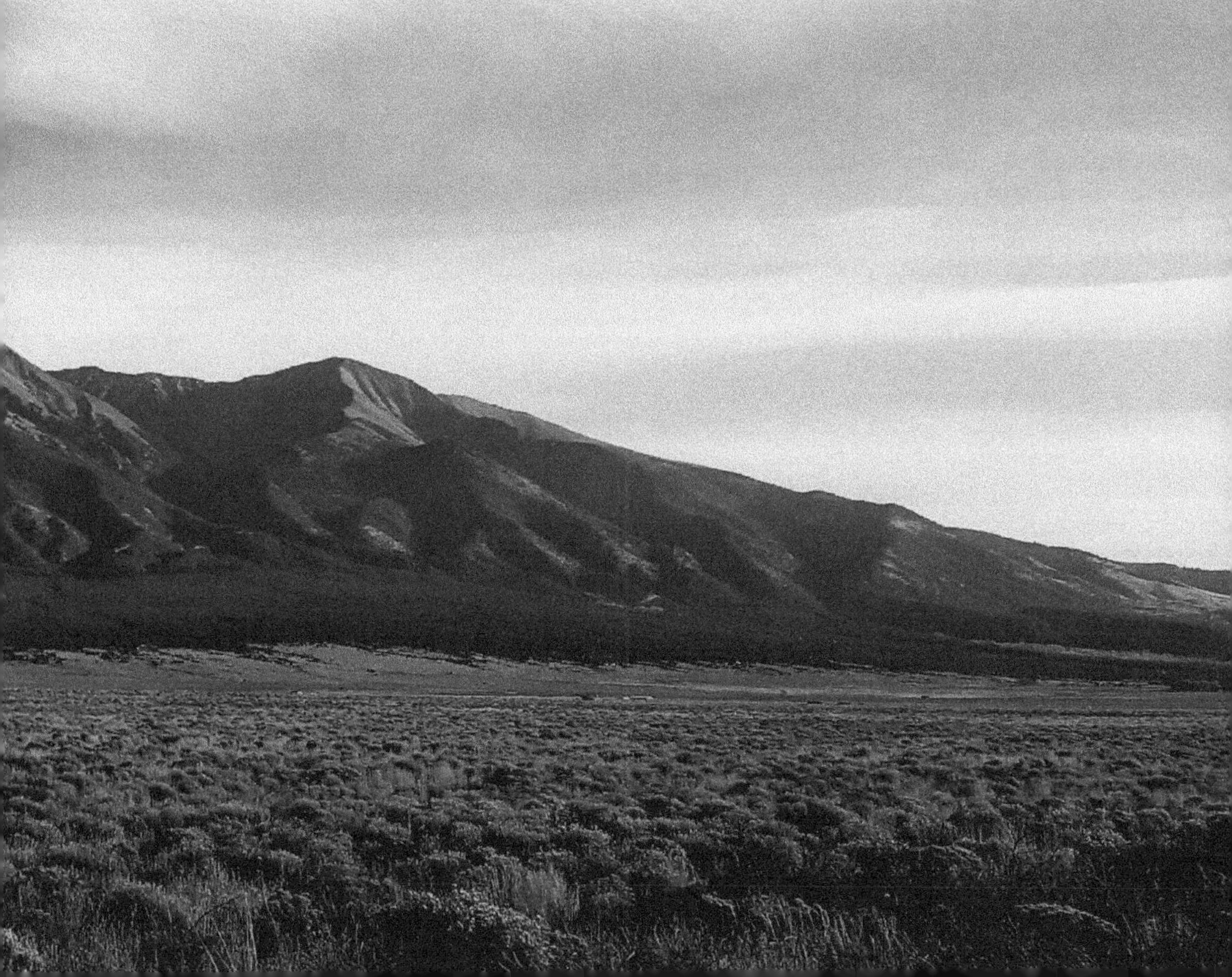

reVision

1. the act of updating or correcting;
2. the act or power of seeing the future with
   renewed imagination or vision.

Eric Carpio

Homelands & Borderlands

> "A border is a dividing line, a narrow strip along a steep edge…a
> vague and undetermined place created by the emotional residue
> of an unnatural boundary. It is in a constant state of transition. The
> prohibited and forbidden are its inhabitants."
> —**Gloria Anzaldúa**, *El otro Mexico*

LOCATED IN SOUTH CENTRAL COLORADO, THE SAN LUIS VALLEY IS HOME
to a unique and memorable landscape. The valley is situated approximately
7,500 feet above sea level and surrounded by picturesque mountain peaks, many
of which are over 14,000 feet. The region embodies environmental borders at the
convergence between the Rocky Mountains and the highest alpine desert in the
United States. Despite being enclosed by the Sangre de Cristo, Sawatch, and
San Juan mountain ranges, the valley contains multiple mountain passes that
have connected the area to adjacent regions for millennia. Among these passes
are La Veta and Mosca Passes to the east, Cochetopa and Poncha Passes to the
north, Wolf Creek Pass to the west, and Cumbres Pass to the south. With an

abundance of natural resources and a diversity of landscapes and ecosystems, the valley has attracted people to, and through, the region for centuries.

The San Luis Valley exists at the intersection of multiple Indigenous homelands and is the traditional hunting grounds of the Ute, the Jicarilla Apache and other Native communities. Towering along the eastern horizon and viewable from just about everywhere in the valley is *Sis Naajiní* (Mount Blanca), Colorado's fourth highest peak and one of four sacred mountains of the Navajo.

As Spain stretched the boundaries of its colonial territory north by establishing settlements in modern-day New Mexico, the San Luis Valley became the northern edge of the early Spanish frontier. As early as the late sixteenth century, the earliest European expeditions entered the valley and the adjacent mountain ranges. In 1694, an expedition led by Don Diego de Vargas traveled through the region. Nearly a century later, in the summer of 1779, Juan Bautista de Anza and an army of nearly 800 soldiers and their allies traveled through the San Luis Valley in search of Cuerno Verde and the Comanche.

In 1821, the Arkansas River, less than 100 miles north of the San Luis Valley, became the border between the United States and Mexico after Mexico gained independence from Spain. For the next twenty-seven years, southern Colorado and the San Luis Valley was situated on the Mexican side of this newly created border region.

Aware that the United States was eyeing expansion to the west, the Mexican government moved to secure their northern border by incentivizing settlements in the region and offering a combination of individual and communal land grants in the San Luis Valley. There were seven Mexican land grants offered in present-day Colorado, exceeding over 8 million acres, and descendants of these land grants continue to live in the valley today.

Manifest Destiny

> "The fulfillment of our manifest destiny to overspread the continent allowed by Providence for the free development of our yearly multiplying millions."
> —**John L. O'Sullivan**, 1845

Inspired by the idea of Manifest Destiny, President James K. Polk was determined to push American territory all the way to the Pacific Ocean. However, thousands of square miles of Mexican territory, including the San Luis Valley, stood in the way.

American annexation of Texas and a border dispute over whether Texas ended at the Nueces River (Mexican claim) or the Rio Grande (U.S. claim), provided Polk with the justification he desired to wage war against Mexico. The war, which Mexicans refer to as the U. S. Invasion, lasted nearly two years (April 1846 to February 1848) and concluded with the signing of the Treaty of Peace, Friendships, Limits, and Settlements, also known as the Treaty of Guadalupe Hidalgo. The treaty shifted the political border south from the Arkansas River in present day Colorado to the current border along the Rio Grande. As a result, the U. S. absorbed nearly 525,000 square miles of cultural borderlands including all or parts of eight states—Arizona, California, Colorado, Nevada, New Mexico, Texas, Utah, and Wyoming.

The treaty had dramatic consequences in the region for generations to come. Magnifying tensions which had been brewing for years, this new geopolitical reality established the region as a site of both conflict and opportunity, between the multiple established indigenous communities, and the increasing number of Americans and Hispanos settling the area and traveling through the region.

Fort Garland

> "It is here that the last wave of Mexican semi-barbarism meets the advancing tide of American progressive civilization, producing as it may be, a clash of languages, laws, and customs, a diversity of mistrust and influence, which renders the presence of military surveillance and police both necessary and judicious."
> —**Kit Carson**, *Report on Fort Garland*, June 1866

Not long after the conclusion of the war, the United States sought to establish control of their new territory by establishing a military presence in the region almost immediately. In 1852, only four years after the signing of the Treaty of Guadalupe Hidalgo, the United States Army made its presence known in the valley by establishing Fort Massachusetts. Fort Massachusetts' location at the base of the Sangre de Cristo Mountains proved to be troublesome, and the Army quickly made plans to find a new location.

On June 24, 1858, soldiers marched six miles south to the newly constructed Fort Garland. Like Fort Massachusetts before it, Fort Garland's mission was to

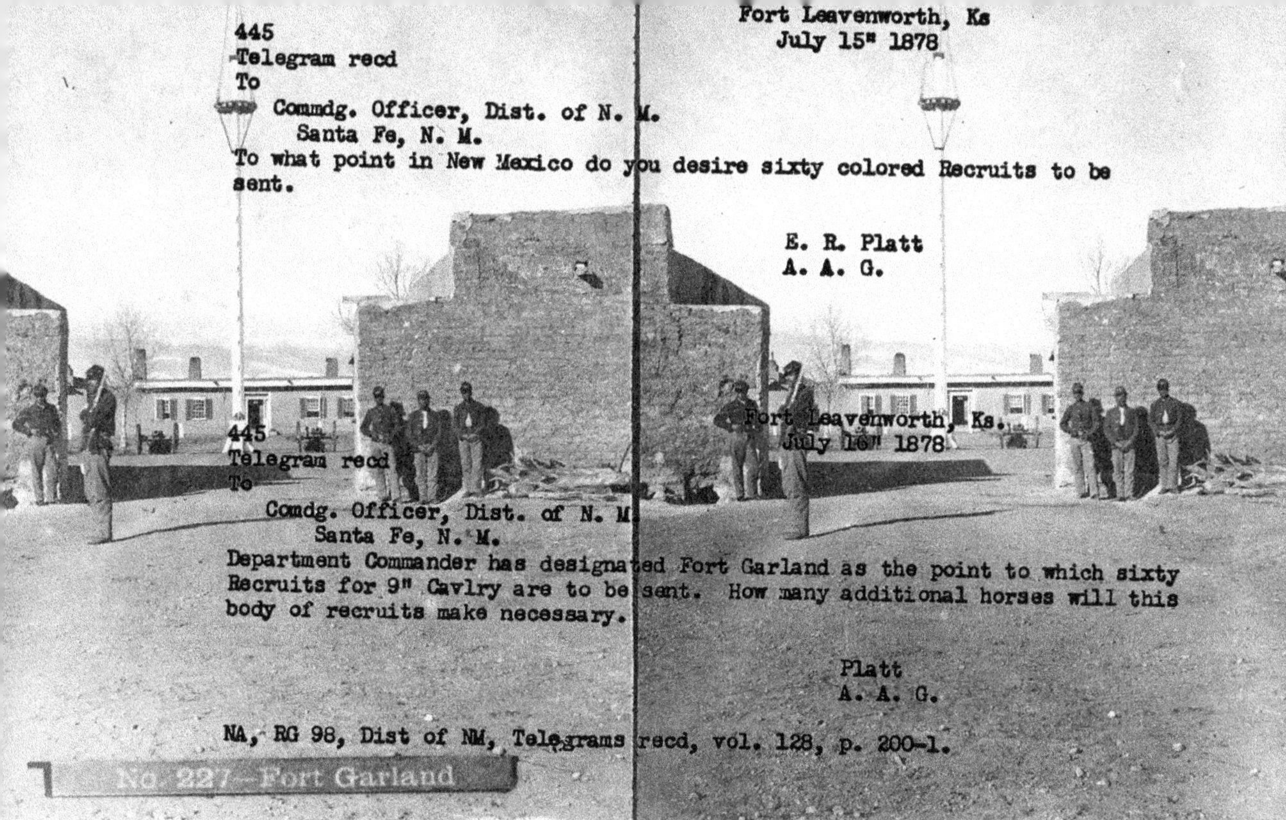

Chip Thomas, *Ninth Cavalry outside Ft. Garland collaged with telegrams regarding disposition of African American troops. c. 1878.* PHOTO OF FORT GARLAND COURTESY HISTORY COLORADO—DENVER, COLORADO

protect a new wave of American, mostly Anglo, settlers and to control and police the valley's Indigenous and Hispano residents. Along with new laws and policies, the Fort Garland period would usher in new conflict and tensions in the region.

Buffalo Soldiers

"We are home now though our flame flickers low. Will you fan it with the winds of freedom, or will you smother it with the sands of humiliation? Will it be that we fought for the lesser of two evils? Or is there this freedom and happiness for all men?"

— **James Harden Daugherty**, World War II Buffalo Soldier

In July of 1866, Congress passed the Army Reorganization Act, establishing six all-Black cavalry and infantry regiments. While African Americans had fought in every prior American military conflict, these units which became known as

Buffalo Soldiers, became the first peacetime regular regiments. Between 1875 and 1879, soldiers in the 9th Cavalry were stationed at Fort Garland.

Early Buffalo Soldier units often consisted of men formerly enslaved. For many Buffalo Soldiers, military service offered one of the few opportunities to provide for themselves and their families. Despite facing significant discrimination and segregation, they were often recognized for serving valiantly and honorably.

Buffalo Soldiers regiments were frequently sent west and assigned to the front lines of the Indian Wars. As the United States pushed westward in its relentless conquest of land, Buffalo Soldiers found themselves serving the country at the expense of Native Americans who had called this land home for millenia.

buffalo soldiers: reVision

The Fort Garland Museum & Cultural Center, a Community Museum of History Colorado, is proud to offer *buffalo soldiers: reVision*, an exhibition at the intersection of history, art, and place, exploring the complex history and legacy of Buffalo Soldiers. Envisioned by lead artist Chip Thomas, aka jetsonorama, and in collaboration with several of the most talented and thoughtful artists across the country, *reVision* disrupts the mythology of the American West through the lens of the Buffalo Soldier experience.

The exhibition critically examines the complexity of the American West in order to understand, acknowledge, and reconcile some of the most painful aspects of our collective history, while updating and expanding our understanding of the Buffalo Soldier legacy. We also view *buffalo soldiers: reVision* as an opportunity to look forward to the future of historical interpretation with renewed perspective and wisdom in order to tell a more honest and inclusive history. ✸

expose large rocks ESTHER BELIN

I knew Slavery was part of the Buffalo Soldiers legacy yet when I dug deeper into my tribal history, I exposed Slavery in my community. I had to reopen the brutality—the physical, cultural, emotional and spiritual soldiering that Slavery played in the conquering of the Frontier. Slavery became another part of the intergenerational trauma I acknowledge.

The many hours viewing the recruitment slogans guaranteeing "FREEDOM, Protection, Pay and a Call to Military Duty," calling many to enlist as "Special Authority Colored Regiments" crushed through the granite boulders placed on top of histories. The shrill messaging is still explosive.

The persona poems idea was to wander into that space where the human soul wonders if those men ached at the genocidal slaughter of Indian men and women. Did they pity those Indians who died to protect their land? I wondered at the idea of property and how the soldiers queried that concept, possibly overhearing conversations that Indians did not feel they owned the land but rather the land was for them to use and be stewards of. I also wondered at the vastness and the climate of the land. How did the soldiers react to the broad spaces, the absence of people and/or infrastructure or dwellings? Did some of the soldiers reconcile with the land? And/or their actions in the role of soldiering in a campaign to slaughter Indians? Did they understand the colonial powers at play in their orders to subjugate Indians?

These are wide and deep inquiries that I started with. I tarried at impasses when large rocks were exposed in the process, perhaps in a similar emotional state to many of these men of color, regarding choice and agency. How do you memorialize the emotional state? How do you intervene the archives, knowing that the archive was created from a settler colonial view? Am I the appropriate person to start those conversations and/or create art around those types of situations?

The poems—historical narrative prose and installation to recreate the emotional impact of the everyday life choices these soldiers made based on the orders they received. I am grieving with issues of race, and the racial imaginary. One of the goals I have for viewers coming to this site is for them to be the witness. I am working to recreate the context of some elements so that we all may understand the complexities, the weight of those gigantic large rocks landmarking great narrative divides.

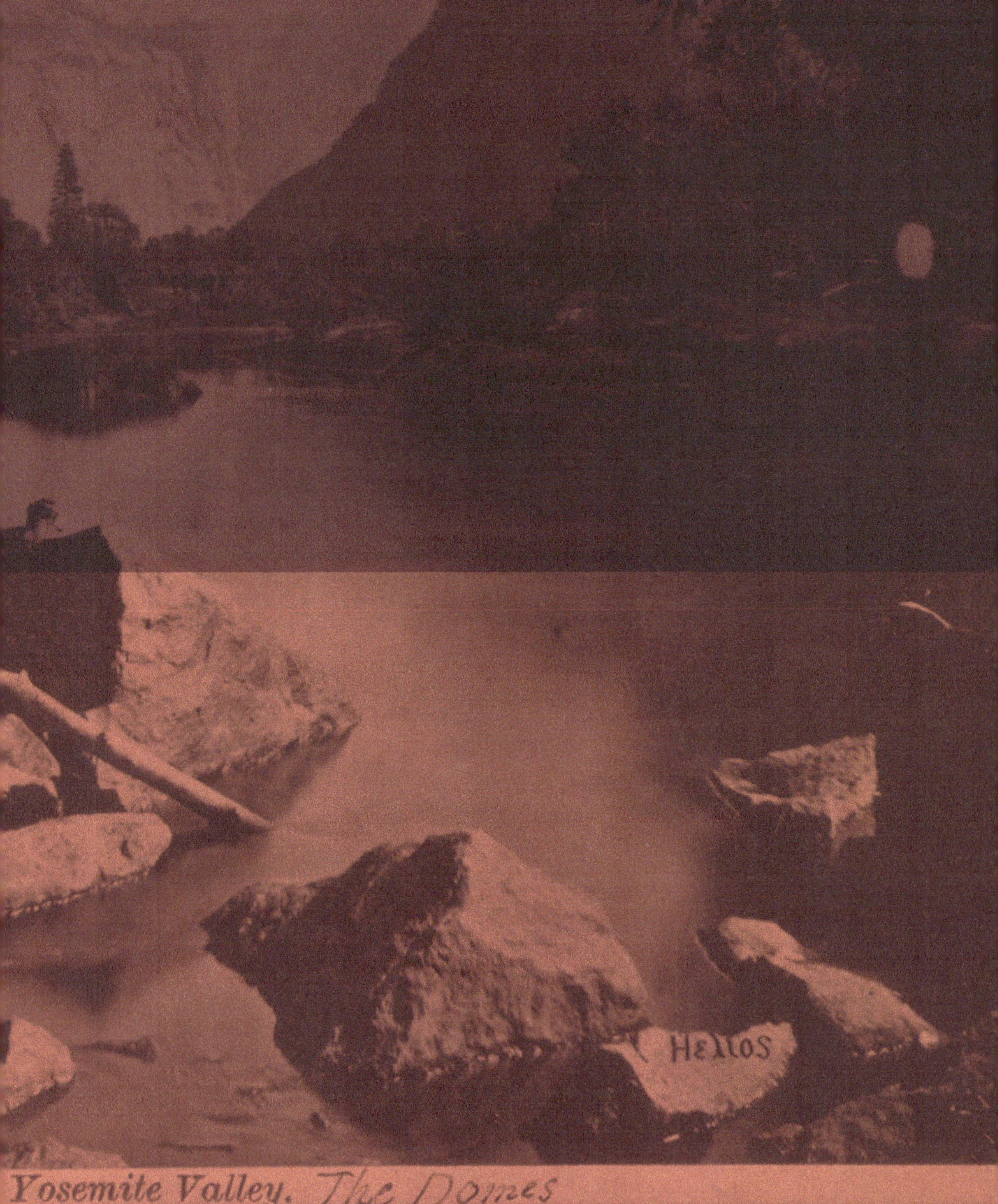

Yosemite Valley. The Domes

meditations on the land

Chip Thomas

THERE IS NO DENYING THAT AS THE UNITED STATES EXPANDED WEST
the Buffalo Soldiers participated in forcing Native people off their land in often
violent and deadly battles. But what was the experience of the African American soldiers in this new landscape? Very few first person accounts from the
U. S. Colored Troops exist today but much has been written about them. Yet
what is written doesn't describe their relationship to or impressions of this
new landscape.

However, we know that as strangers in a foreign land Buffalo Soldiers were
also responsible for exploring and mapping vast parts of the western frontier
such as the New Mexico Territory. "Their maps identified mountain ranges,
peaks, land elevations, and deadly areas like White Sands. They marked the
boundaries of military and Indian reservations and identified travel, mail, and
military routes."[1] In this capacity the soldiers were also involved in protecting
and building the infrastructure on unceded Native land and in protecting those
western tribes on reservation land.

President Ulysses S. Grant signed the Act of March 1, 1872, which established Yellowstone National Park as a public park or pleasuring ground for the
benefit and enjoyment of the people."[2] This did not include Native people. In

André Leon Gray,
Indian Land for $ale.
Letterpress print,
oil-based ink on
archival paper, 13 x 19",
2022

INDIAN
LAND
FOR
SALE

1890 Sequoia and General Grant National Parks were established. Because there was no one to protect the parks settler farmers and ranchers would enter freely and frequently to graze animals and collect timber with little regard for the landscape or wildlife. Wanting to protect these resources the government's response was to have Army troops stationed nearby patrol the parks. Approximately 500 Buffalo Soldiers served as Park Rangers at Yosemite, Sequoia and General Grant National Parks, in 1899, 1903 and 1904 where their duties included evicting cattle grazers, sheepherders, timber thieves, putting out forest fires and building roads and trails.

In 1903, African American 9th Cavalry Captain Charles Young became the acting superintendent of Sequoia National Park. Along with the 9th Cavalry, their efforts at the Sequoia "to protect the land by preserving vegetation and stopping erosion helped diffuse some of the racist perceptions of local whites towards the African American soldiers,"[3] notes historian Brian Shellum.

The land west of the Mississippi River became a focal point for conflicting ways of being in the land. The Native way of nurturing the land and living in balance with its offerings was juxtaposed with the western desire to conquer and own the land. In this sense the land wasn't shared by the different races on the frontier but there were moments of shared experiences and moments of shared beauty and awe of being in the land.

Did the endless horizon of the western sky or the millions of stars in the nighttime sky inspire the formerly enslaved soldiers to dream of new realities beyond their wildest imaginings? Did being in the land bring them peace? Was there amongst the U.S. Colored Troops a black doppelganger of Everett Ruess whose heart would burst if he experienced even one more day of beauty in the western landscape? ❋

ENDNOTES
1. *Buffalo Soldiers on the Colorado Frontier.* Nancy K. Williams, 2021. Page 105.
2. https://www.history.com/news/buffalo-soldiers-national-parks-rangers
3. Ibid.

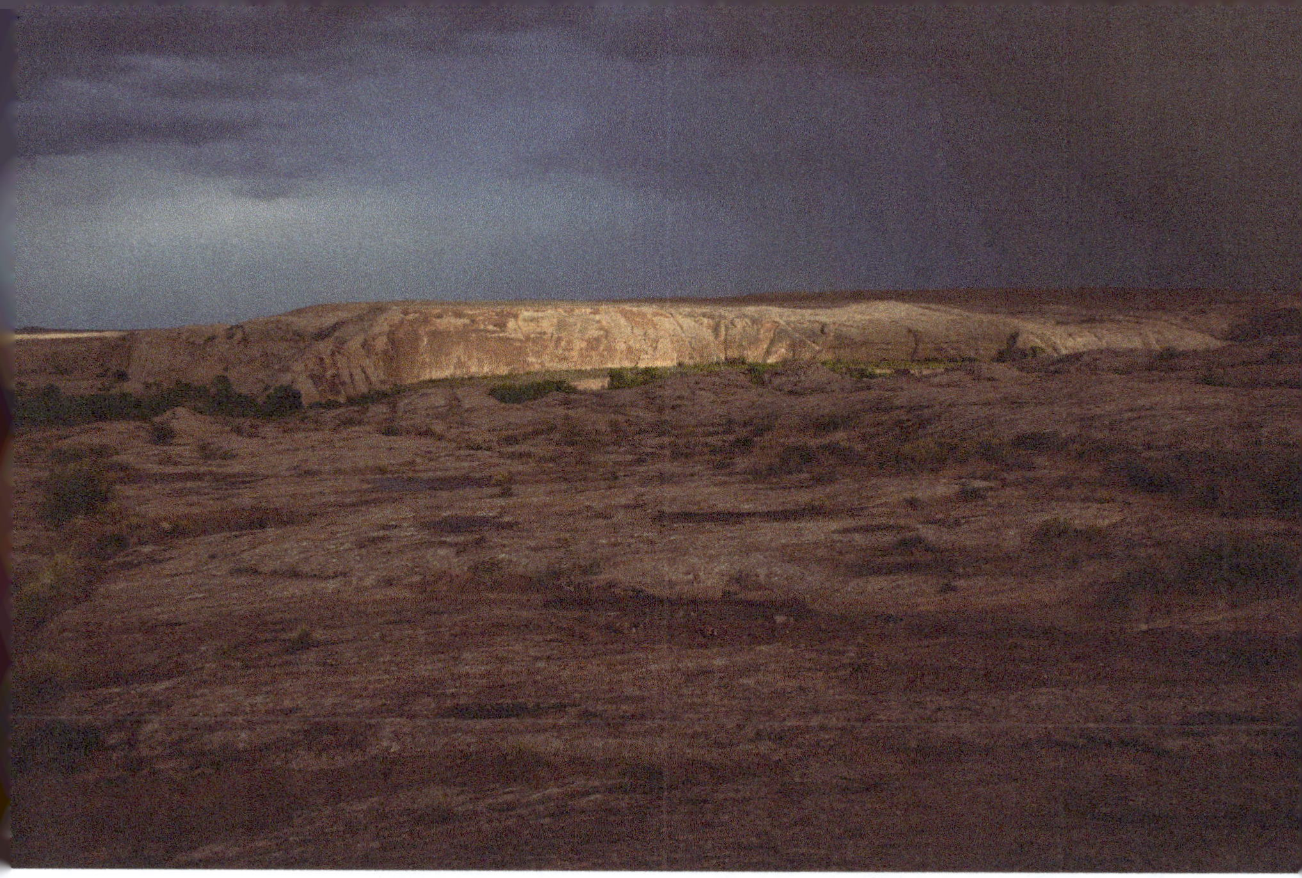

Chip Thomas, *after the storm.*
Digital photograph, 2013

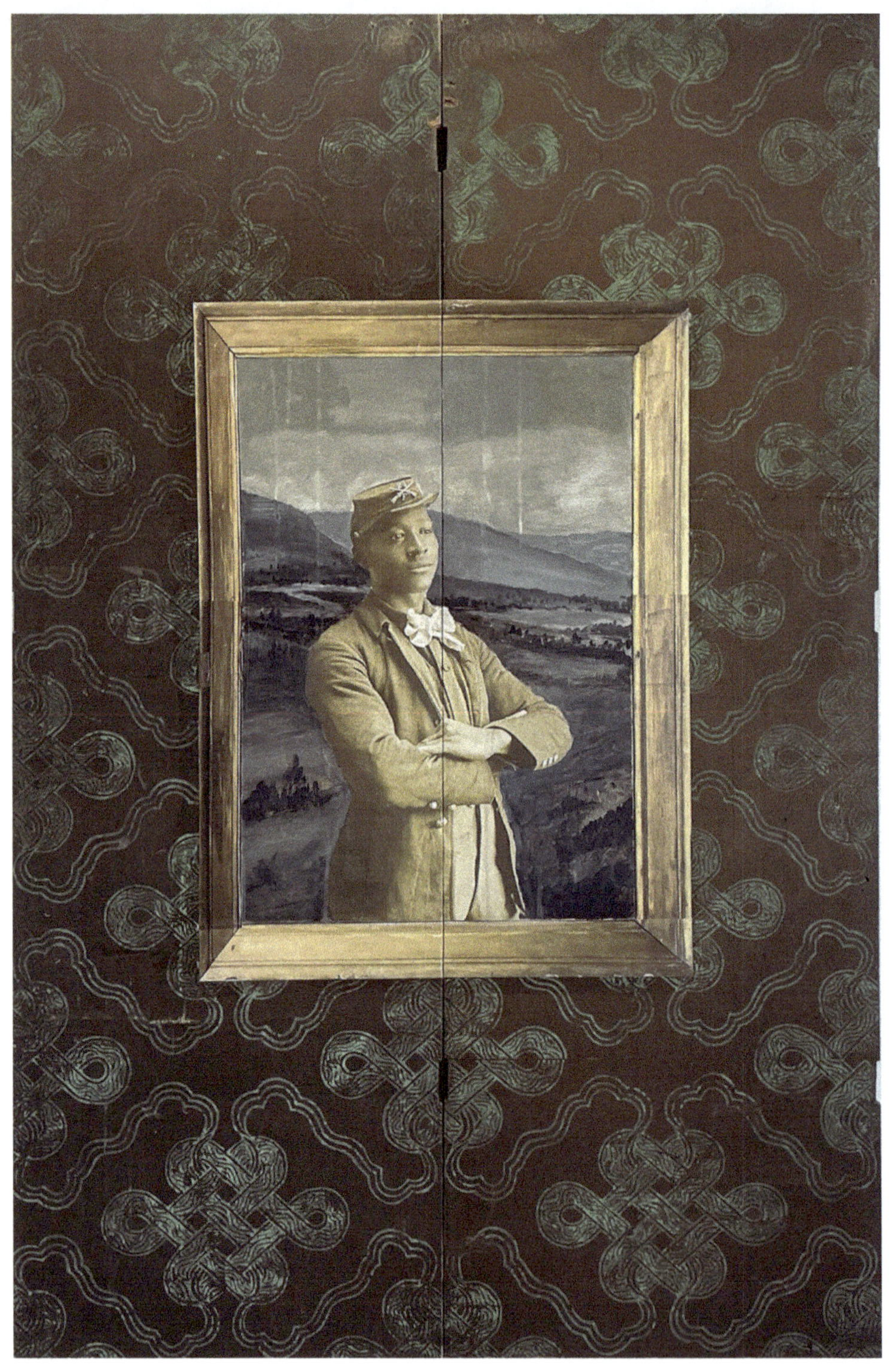

Tom Judd, *Buffalo Soldier #1.*
Mixed media on found screen,
58 x 27" 2022

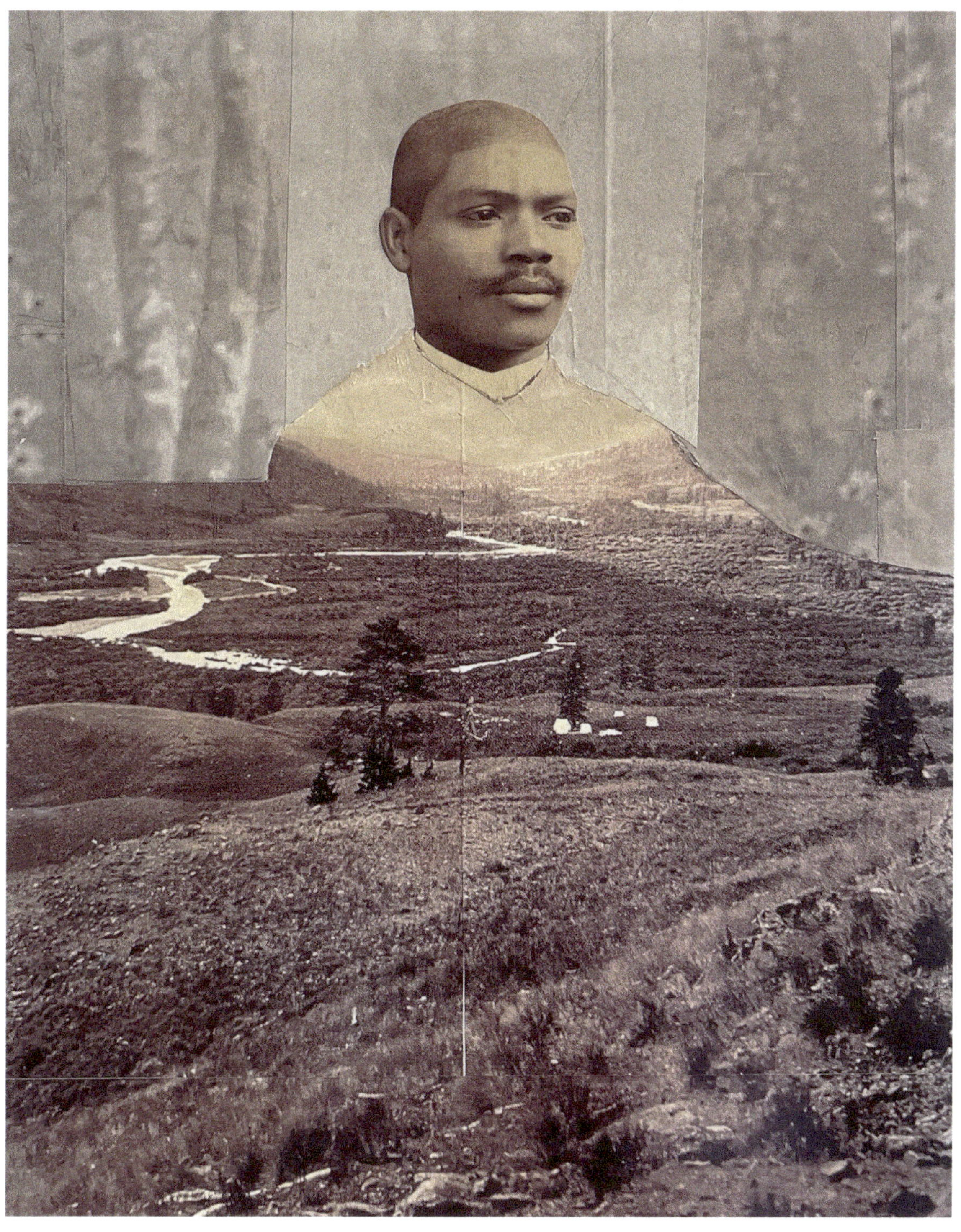

Tom Judd, *The Returning*. Mixed
media on panel, 30 x 23", 2023

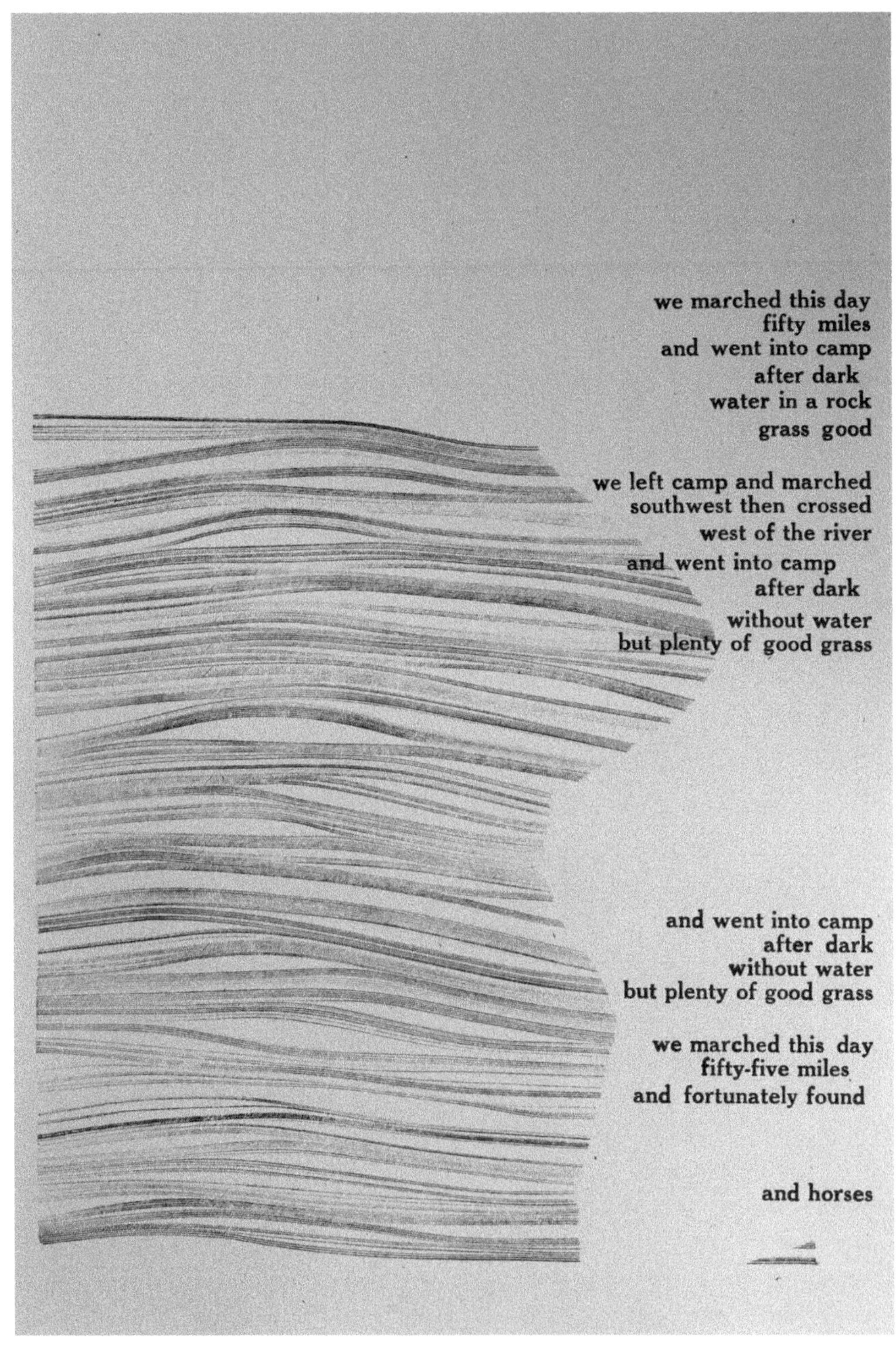

Rosie Carter, *Buffalo soldier's journal entry.*
Letterpress prints, oil-based ink on
archival paper, 12.5 x 19", 2022

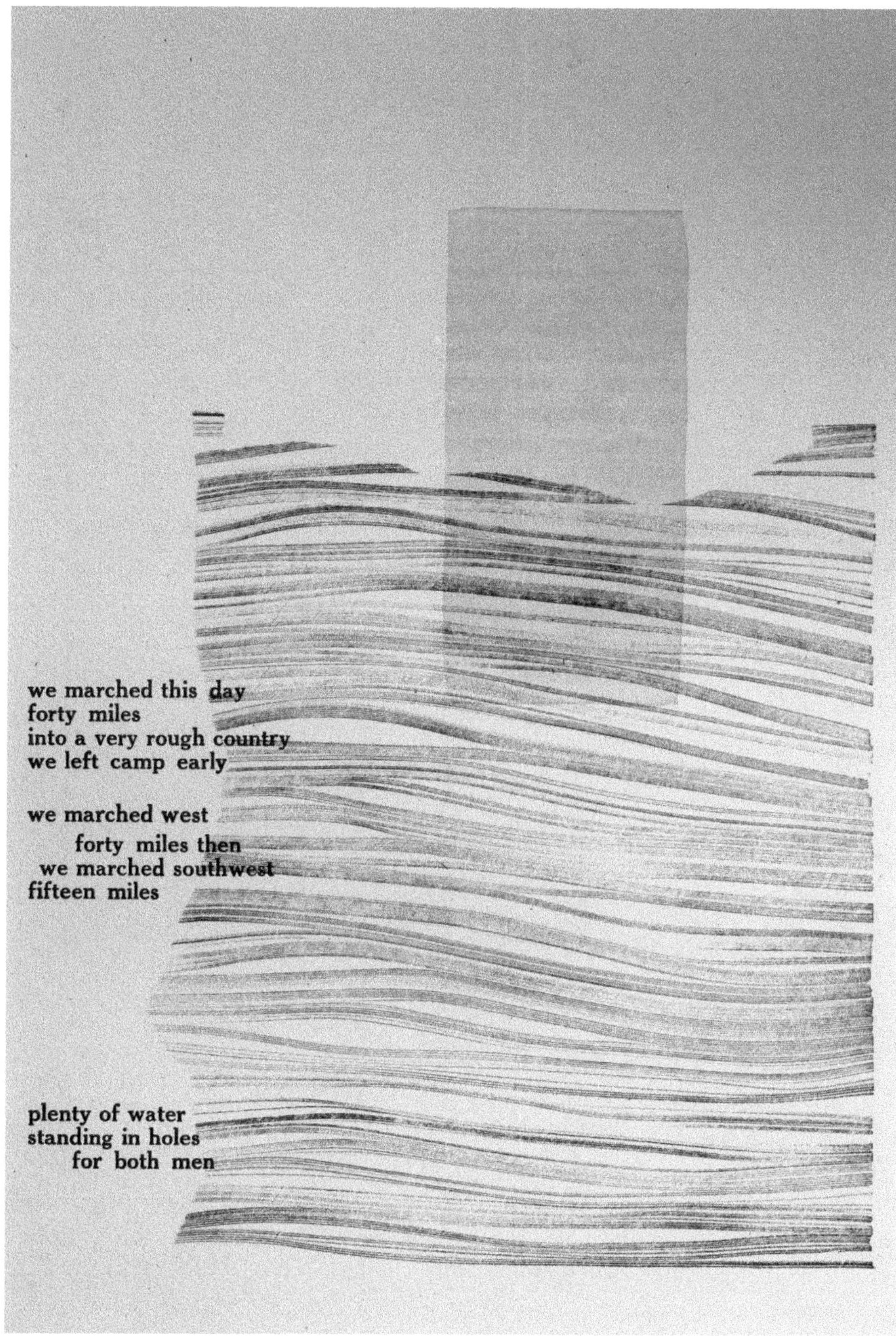

we marched this day
forty miles
into a very rough country
we left camp early

we marched west
      forty miles then
  we marched southwest
fifteen miles

plenty of water
standing in holes
      for both men

how to divide a land into a nation

Rosie Carter

We gouge.
We blast and drill,
Plow, berm and tunnel.
We scrape and scratch at the surface
As if trying to get in.
And when all that fails we pull it apart,
Identifying layers of rock
As strata. As anticlines, synclines
And sedimentary infill.
Like parts of a sandwich
And not, in actuality,
Earth.

Or we dissect it ephemerally,
Imposing imagined lines
Of territories,
Nations, states and townships.
Where there is, in truth,
Only the intact surface
Of a dense mineral ball.
A ball suspended in space
By the mere magic
Of gravity.

Why does this thing in our minds
Need to be separated from the reality
That it is,
From every standpoint or perspective,
From every which way you squint,
Or try looking at it sideways the dark,
The very planet

Known as the speck in the universe
That is home?

Make no mistake
My fellow white European descendants,
I'm speaking of us.
My blue eyes and my ancestors
Are inescapable markers of a legacy
Of stealing land from its indigenous people.
Of erecting fences and forts.
Of surveying and splintering
And reducing to remnants.

Have you not seen the homestead maps?
160 acres square lined up proper in 1862,
An infestation of identical boxes back to back.
The dividing lines are so rigid and weird.
Drawn for efficient fragmentation,
For organized appropriation.
How could they ever fit
The contours of a river bank
Or dense foliage of a forest?

COME ON you men ensconced in chambers,
Have you never smelled sage after a rain?
Or watched sun dapple a forest when the fog has lifted?
Do you not know that land has a life of its own?
A life tethered to a people. To plants,
Rocks, rivers, air and animals.
Life that didn't know
A violent dissection and thievery
Would someday carve
The gully sculpted hills.
The cloud swathed mountains.

And where amongst the branches
Of the human family tree
Did my ancestors conceive of the world
In parts?

Where were we when it went
From vast to plots?
Did its immenseness frighten us?
Were we afraid of what lay beyond the horizon?
Did we fool ourselves into thinking to dissect,
To possess,
To own a small part of the unknowable
Would make us safe?
As if it's possible to escape the dark,
To save ourselves from illness and car crash.

So here's the question:
Does possession inherently mean dissection?
Does a thing need to be broken into pieces
Small enough to be gripped in a hand?
Clenched tightly in a fist?
Land, for instance,
A thing broad and wide and far as the eye can see,
Must it be measured and mapped,
Fenced and fortified,
In order to be grasped?

Because this carving up and
Clenching tight
Has only led to heartache.
It's only led to divisions and alienations.
To genocide and justifications.
At best it's left us hollow inside.
At worst, missing and murdered.
What we've done to land, we've done to others.
And every day we act as if
This dividing and conquering
Is the only way forward.
As if this frail filament of an idea,
Fraught and caught in the
Immense web of humanity
Must always
Hold us
Hostage ✳

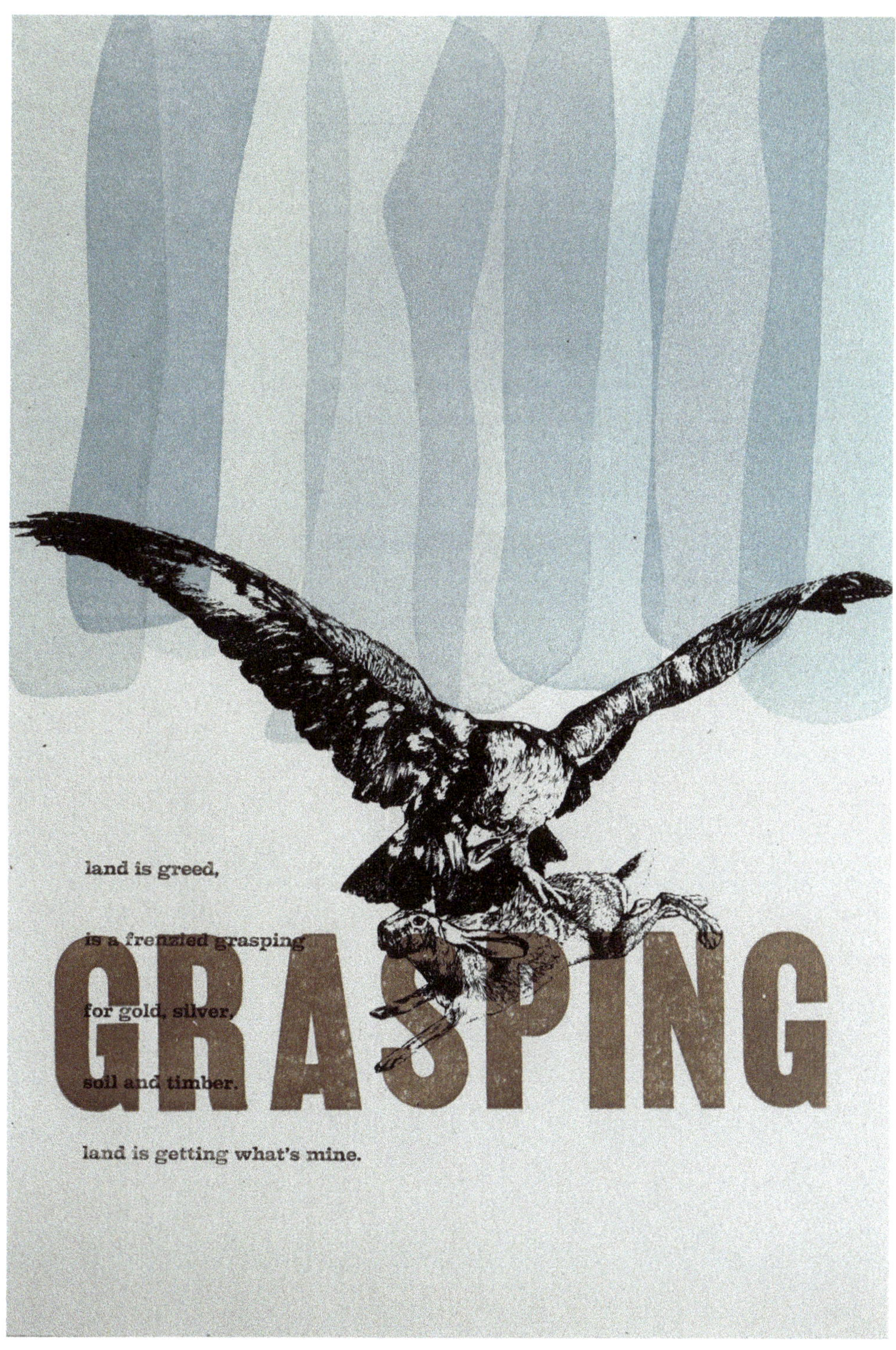

Rosie Carter, *Grasping*. Letterpress and screen print, oil and water-based inks on archival paper, 12.5 x 19", 2023

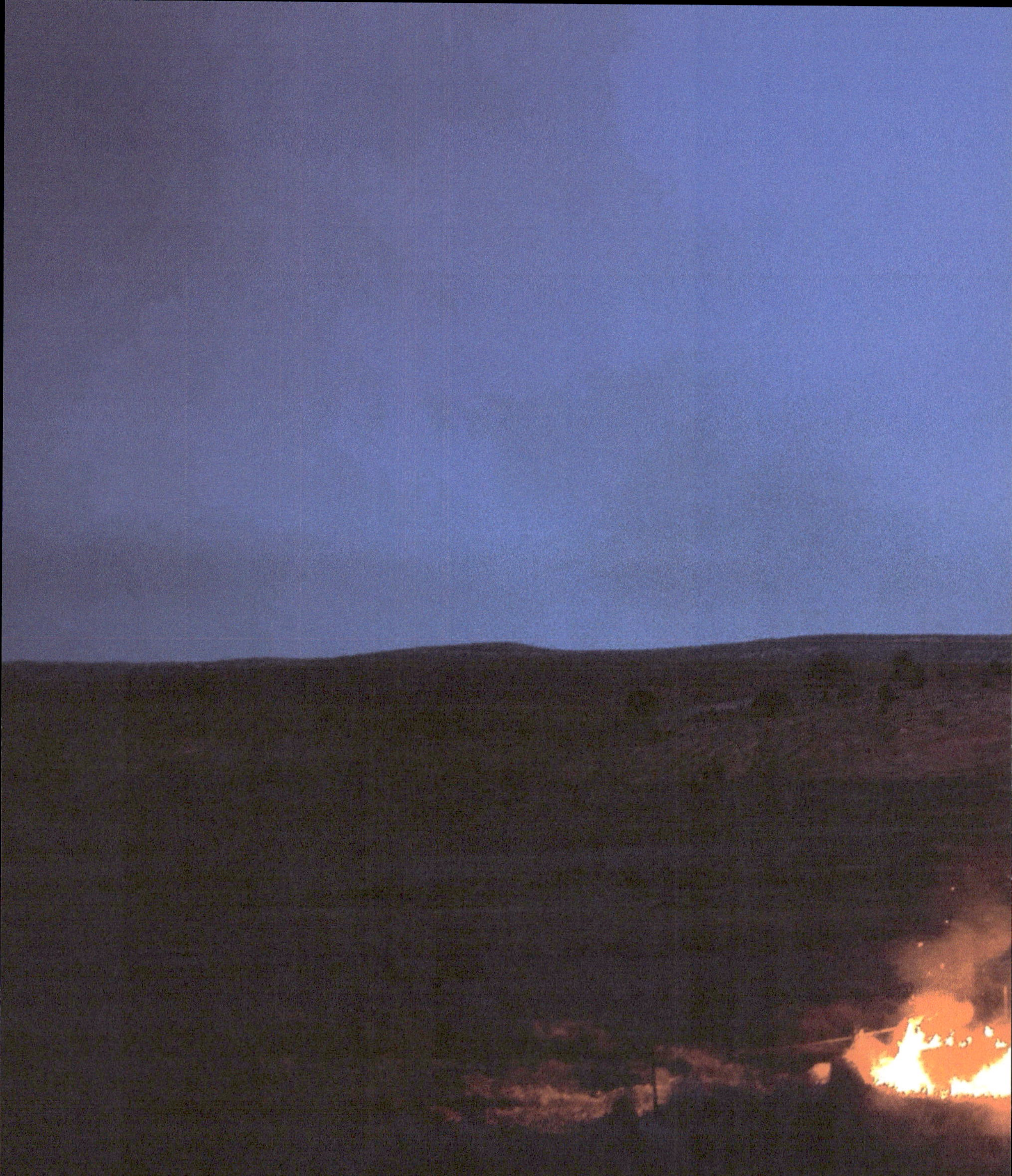

twenty fifth infantry regiment bicycle corps

How Buffalo Soldiers were employed to test the combat viability of bicycles

Chip Thomas

BY THE LATE 1800S BICYCLES WERE BEGINNING TO HAVE A MOMENT. Affordable and efficient, they provided autonomy for riders. Initially, tires were made of metal bands on wooden rims, which didn't wear well and produced bumpy, uncomfortable riding conditions. But in the late 1880s, Scottish inventor John Dunlop modified the pneumatic tire, which had been developed few decades previously, but which had failed to take off. The primary source of rubber for these tires came from King Leopold's Congo Free State. Because of the atrocities associated with the collection of this rubber, it was called "red rubber."[1]

By the 1880s bicycles were being used by the military in Europe and in the United States. "Bikes proved less expensive and easier to maintain than the horses typically used by the cavalry."[2]

Civil War and Indian Wars veteran Nelson A. Miles emerged as a key advocate for using bikes in the Army. "Following the example of the First Signal of the Connecticut National Guard, which in 1891 became the first American unit to formally utilize bicycles, Miles authorized several trials to determine the effectiveness of the new mode of transportation, including relay teams that delivered messages from Chicago to New York and Washington, D.C. to Denver."[3]

Cover of Spalding athletic library issue. COURTESY BEINECKE RARE BOOK AND MANUSCRIPT LIBRARY, YALE UNIVERSITY LIBRARY

PREVIOUS SPREAD
Chip Thomas, *brush fires in the social landscape—after wojnarowicz.* Digital photograph, 2017

Vol. 6, No. 62.
Issued Monthly.

FEBRUARY, 1897.

Price, 10 Cents.
$1.20 per Year.

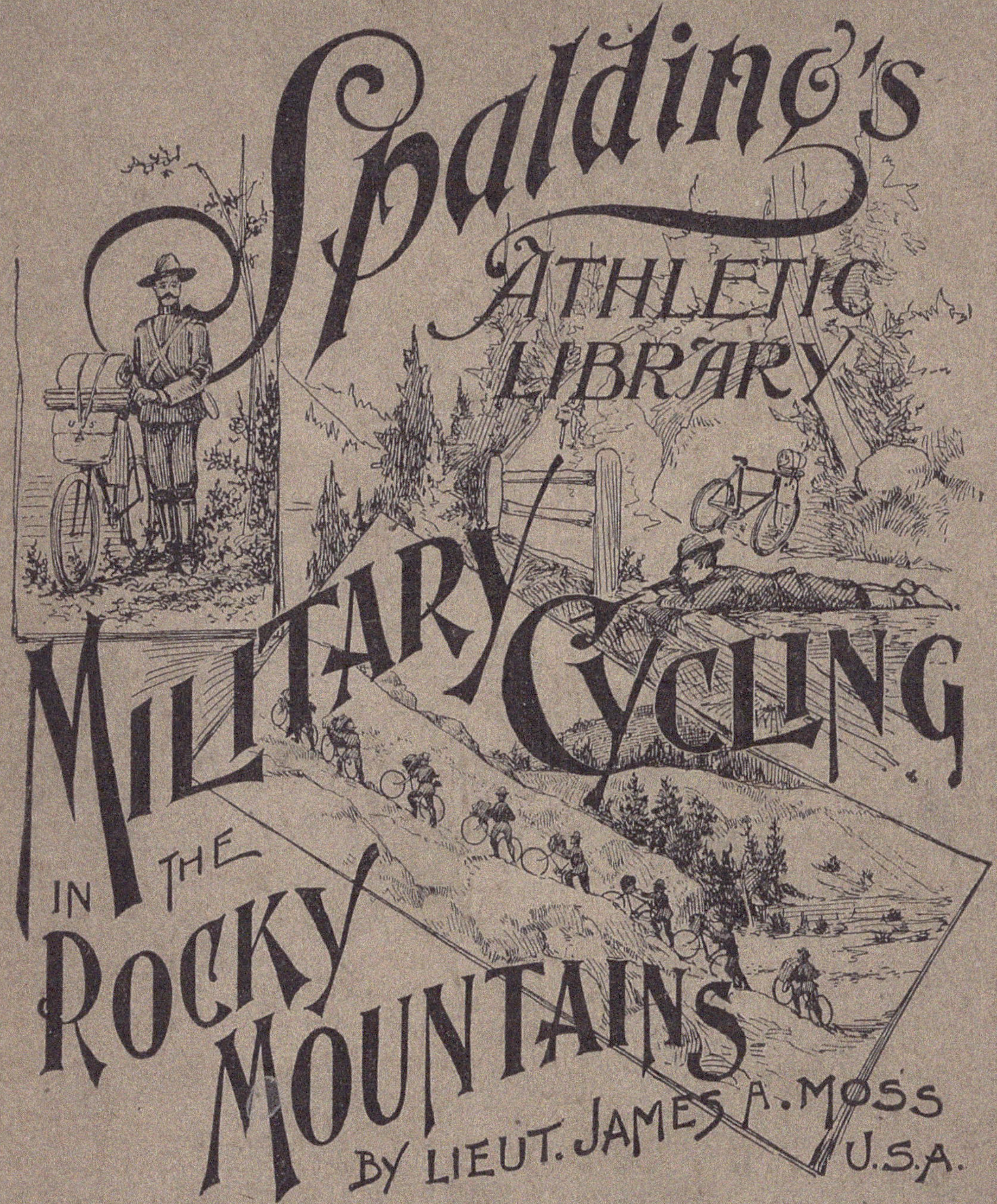

PUBLISHED BY THE
AMERICAN SPORTS PUBLISHING CO.
241 BROADWAY, NEW YORK.

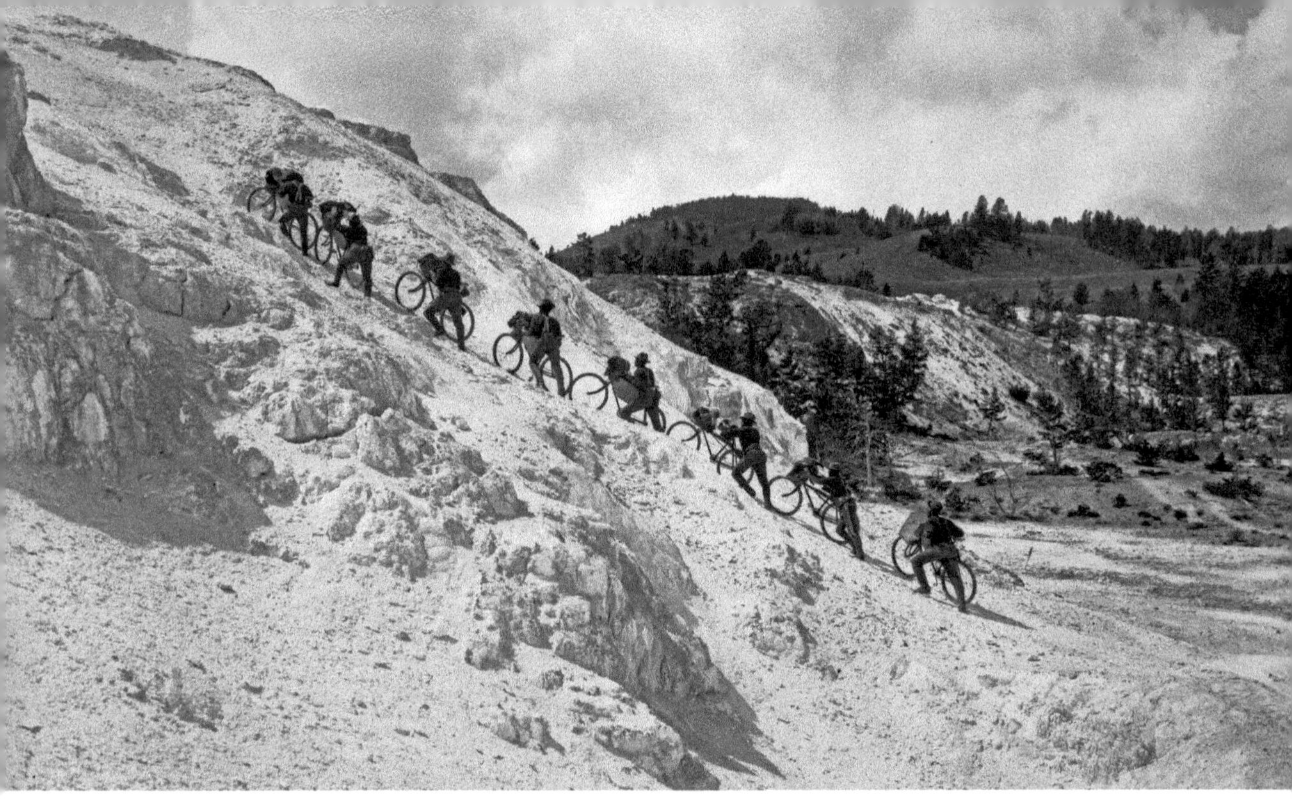

Recent West Point graduate James A. Moss was a new lieutenant general at Fort Missoula who was also a cycling enthusiast. He proposed to Miles that he train a contingent of the 25th Infantry to perform a long-distance mission to test the efficacy of the bicycles and the stamina of the soldiers. Miles approved the request.

In August 1896 their first long training ride was a round trip expedition from Fort Missoula to Yellowstone National Park some 275 miles away. The bicycle sponsor for these expeditions was the A.G. Spalding Company and Brothers. The men covered 796 miles in 126 hours on fixed gear bicycles weighing 80 pounds. It was on this training ride that the classic Minerva Terrace photos were taken.

This ride a success, the soldiers continued training the duration of 1896 for a 1900 mile expedition from Fort Missoula to St. Louis, Missouri. They left Fort Missoula June 14, 1897 and arrived 41 days later to a hero's reception in St. Louis on July 17th. The riders included: John Findley, Elwood Forman, William Haynes, Frank L. Johnson, William Proctor Sergeant Mingo Sanders (veteran of the Spanish American War and the Philippines War, who in 1906 was falsely

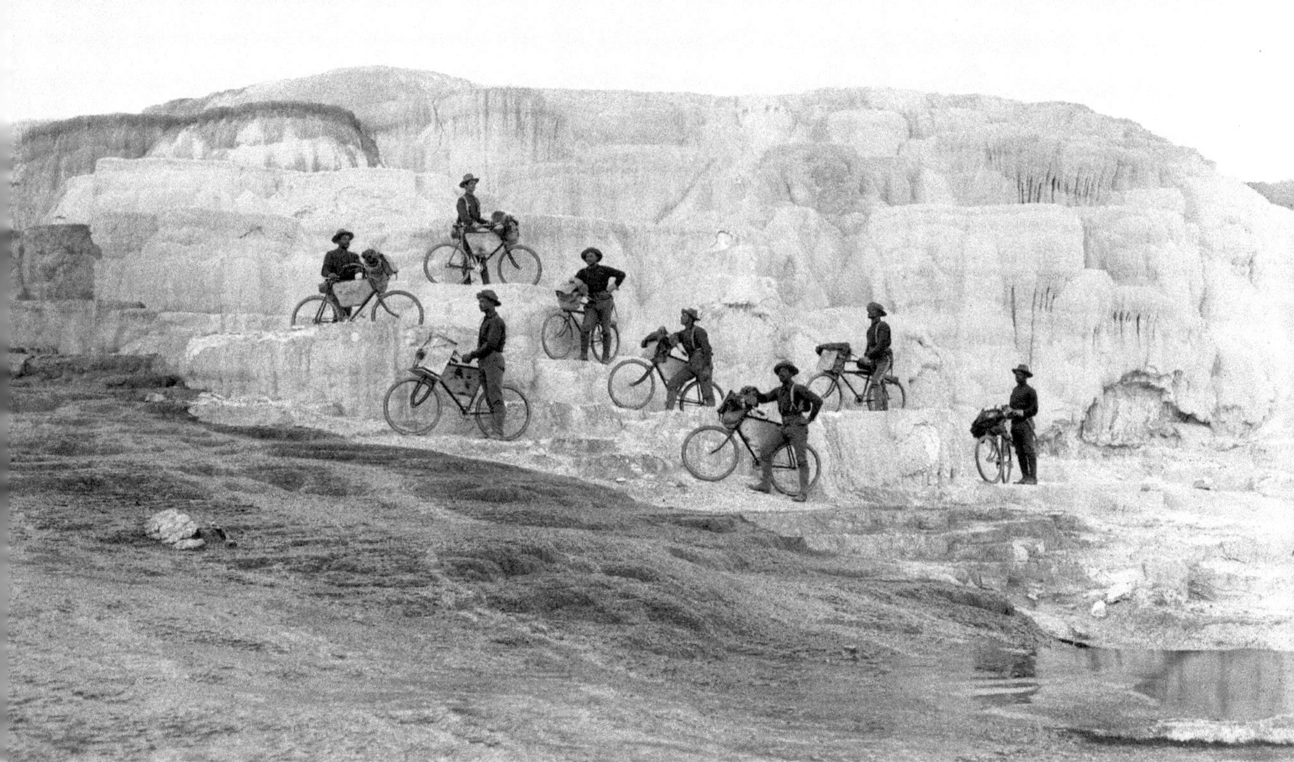

Bicycle Corps on Minerva Terrace in Yellowstone National Park, 1896. COURTESY HAYNES FOUNDATION COLLECTION, MONTANA HISTORICAL SOCIETY

indicted in the Brownsville Affray along with 125 other Buffalo Soldiers), Lieutenant Corporal Abram Martin, musician Elias Johnson, and privates George Scott, Hiram L. B. Dingman, Travis Bridges, John Cook, Richard Rout, Eugene Jones, Sam Johnson, William Williamson, Sam Williamson, John H. Wilson, Samuel Reid, and Francis Button. ❈

ENDNOTES
1. https://shorturl.at/fyBWX
2. https://www.smithsonianmag.com/history/the-black-buffalo-soldiers
   -who-biked-across-the-american-west-180980246/
3. Ibid.

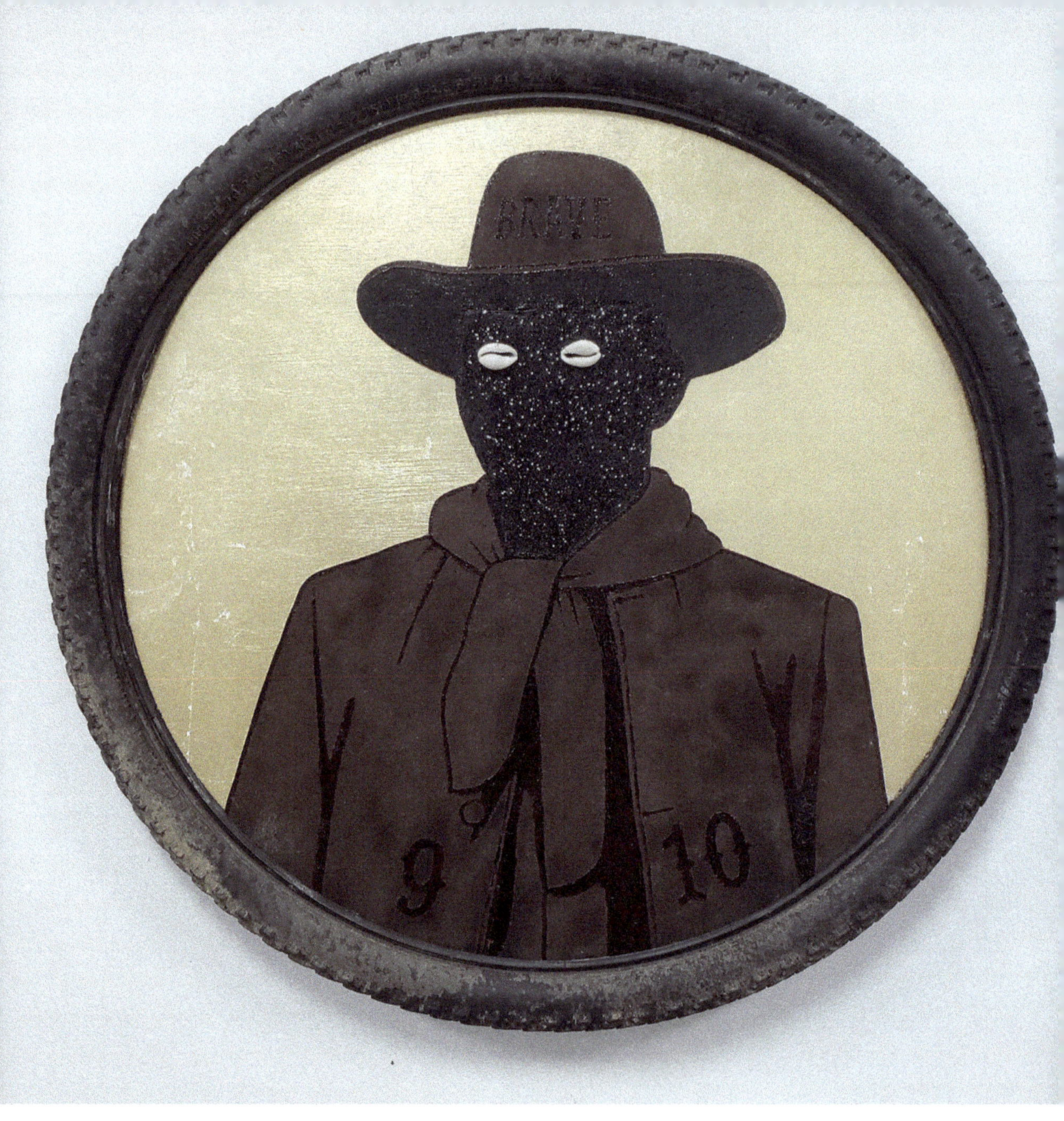

André Leon Gray, *Fighting in the land of the free, while desiring a better future.* Tar, black glitter, and cowrie shells on canvas with gold leaf on MDF, raw cotton, and soil on reclaimed bicycle tire, 26" diameter, 2023

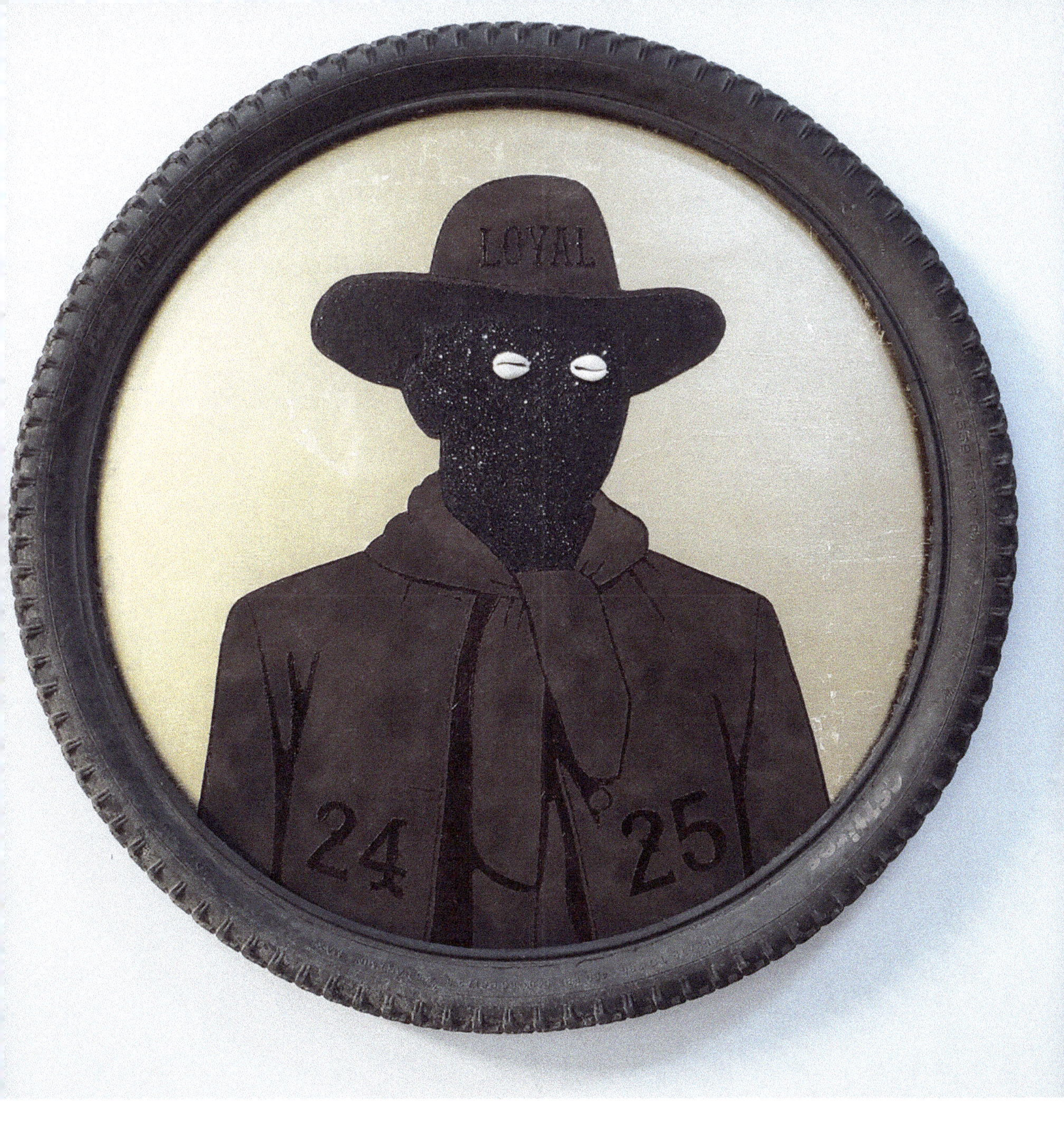

André Leon Gray, *Defending the disrupters as he looked into the infinite*. Tar, black glitter, and cowrie shells on canvas with gold leaf on MDF, raw cotton, and soil on reclaimed bicycle tire, 26" diameter, 2023

propaganda in the press, print media and popular culture

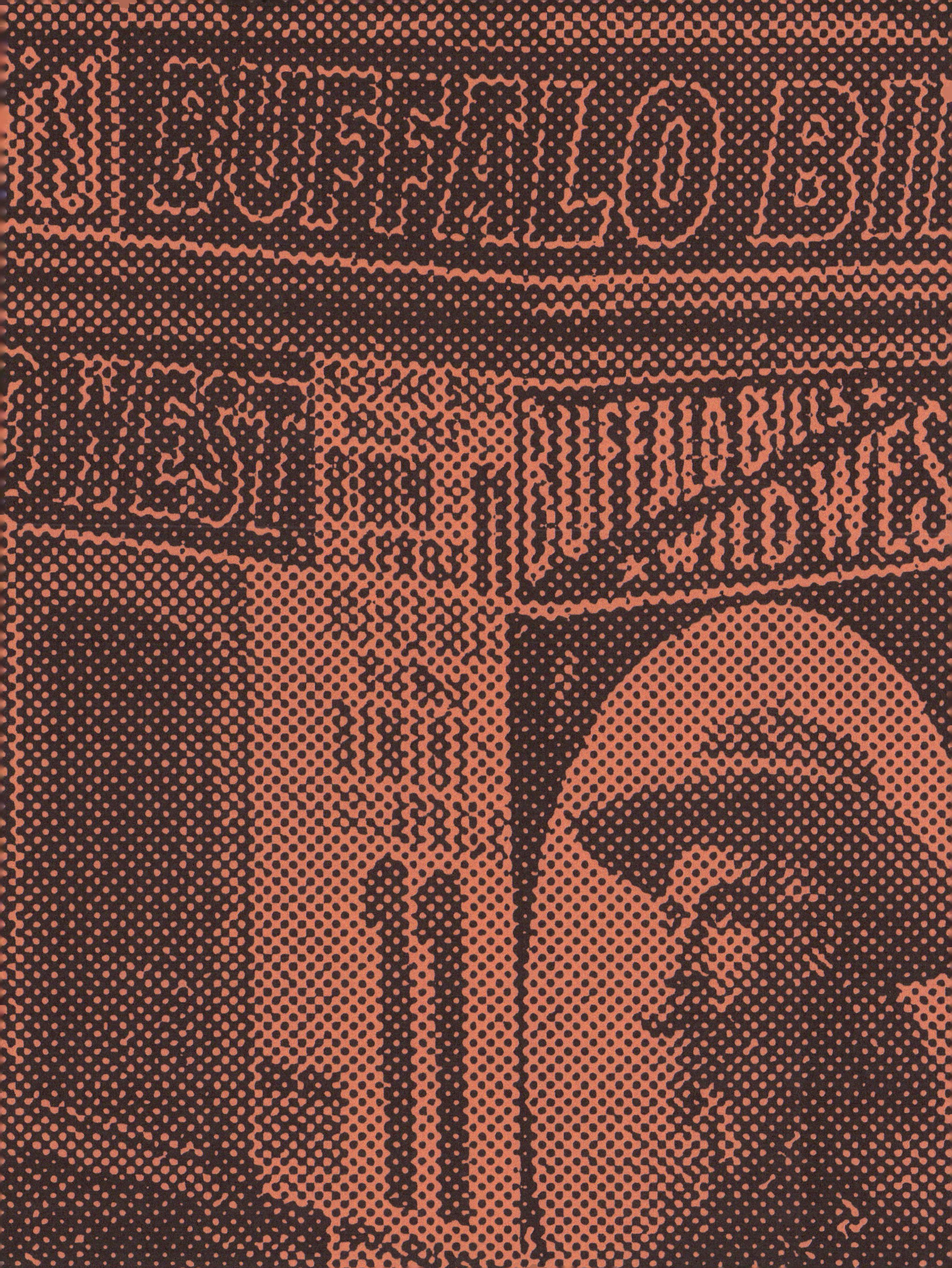

Chip Thomas

Chip Thomas,
Whipped Peter,[1]
collage, inkjet print,
20 x 30", 2023.
WHIPPED PETER,
LILJENQUIST FAMILY
COLLECTION, LIBRARY
OF CONGRESS; MEN OF
COLOR TO ARMS! NOW
OR NEVER, THE ALFRED
WHITAL STERN
COLLECTION OF
LINCOLNIANA

REVIEWING PERIOD SPECIFIC RECRUITMENT ADS FOR THE MILITARY and public references to anti-blackness in the late 1800s provides an opportunity to experience imagery Black people may have seen when they went to town. This imagery gives insight into factors influencing enslaved people to escape and seek a better life. Though most enslaved people were illiterate perhaps they overheard conversations amongst white people of Black men being recruited into the Union army and later into the U. S. Colored troops.

Concomitantly, the visual landscape was also plastered with large broadsides announcing the P. T. Barnum Circus and Buffalo Bill's Wild West. Perhaps more than any other form of media during the 34 years that Buffalo Bill toured his Wild West show in the United States and Europe(1883–1917), his advertising shaped the narrative of ascendent civilization, manifest destiny and the static stereotypical notion of Native people as savages and having been eliminated.

As an African American man who has spent the last 36 years living and working as a physician on the Navajo nation, a recurring question for me regarding the Buffalo Soldiers' involvement in the Indian Wars is why? What motivated men who were formerly enslaved, many of whom escaped slavery and fought in the Civil War to participate in the Indian Wars?

1. https://www
   .history.com
   /news/whipped
   -peter-slavery
   -photo-scourged
   -back-real
   -story-civil-war

MEN OF COLOR

TO ARMS! TO ARMS!

NOW OR NEVER

This is our golden moment!   The Government of the United States calls for every Able-bodied Colored Man to enter the Army for the

Three Years' Service!

And join in Fighting the Battles of Liberty and the Union.   A new era is open to us.   For generations we have suffered under the horrors of slavery, outrage and wrong; our manhood has been denied, our citizenship blotted out, our souls seared and burned, our spirits cowed and crushed, and the hopes of the future of our race involved in doubt and darkness.   But now our relations to the white race are changed.   Now, therefore, is our most precious moment.   Let us rush to arms!

FAIL NOW, & OUR RACE IS DOOMED

On this the soil of our birth.   We must now awake, arise, or be forever fallen.   If we value liberty, if we wish to be free in this land, if we love our country, if we love our families, our children, our home, we must strike now while the country calls; we must rise up in the dignity of our manhood, and show by our own right arms that we are worthy to be freemen.   Our enemies have made the country believe that we are craven cowards, without soul, without manhood, without the spirit of soldiers.   Shall we die with this stigma resting upon our graves?   Shall we leave this inheritance of Shame to our Children?   No! a thousand times NO!   We WILL Rise!   The alternative is upon us.   Let us rather die freemen than live to be slaves.   What is life without liberty?   We say that we have manhood: now is the time to prove it.   A nation or a people that cannot fight may be pitied, but cannot be respected.   If we would be regarded men, if we would forever silence the tongue of Calumny, of Prejudice and hate, let us Rise Now and Fly to Arms!   We have seen what Valor and Heroism our Brothers displayed at Port Hudson and Milliken's Bend, though they are just from the galling, poisoning grasp of Slavery, they have startled the World by the most exalted heroism.   If they have proved themselves heroes, cannot WE PROVE OURSELVES MEN?

ARE FREEMEN LESS BRAVE THAN SLAVES

More than a Million White Men have left Comfortable Homes and joined the Armies of the Union to save their Country.   Cannot we leave ours, and swell the Hosts of the Union, to save our liberties, vindicate our manhood, and deserve well of our Country.   MEN OF COLOR! the Englishman, the Irishman, the Frenchman, the German, the American, have been called to assert their claim to freedom and a manly character, by an appeal to the sword.   The day that has seen an enslaved race in arms has, in all history, seen their last trial.   We now see that our last opportunity has come.   If we are not lower in the scale of humanity than Englishmen, Irishmen, White Americans and other Races, we can show it now.   Men of Color, Brothers and Fathers, we appeal to you, by all your concern for yourselves and your liberties, by all your regard for God and humanity, by all your desire for Citizenship and Equality before the law, by all your love for the Country, to stop at no subterfuge, listen to nothing that shall deter you from rallying for the Army.   Come Forward, and at once Enroll your Names for the Three Years' Service.   Strike now, and you are henceforth and forever Freemen!

E. D. Bassett,	Rev. J. Underdue,	P. J. Armstrong,	Rev. J. C. Gibbs,	Elijah J. Davis,
William D. Forten.	John W. Price,	J. W. Simpson.	Daniel George,	John P. Burr,
Frederick Douglass.	Augustus Dorsey,	Rev. J. B. Trusty,	Robert M. Adger,	Robert Jones,
Wm. Whipper,	Rev. Stephen Smith,	S. Morgan Smith,	Henry M. Cropper,	O. V. Catto,
D. D. Turner,	N. W. Depee,	William E. Gipson,	Rev. J. B. Reeve,	Thos. J. Dorsey,
Jas. McCrummell.	Dr. J. H. Wilson,	Rev. J. Boulden.	Rev. J. A. Williams,	I. D. Cliff,
A. S. Cassey,	J. W. Cassey,	Rev. J. Asher,	Rev. A. L. Stanford.	Jacob C. White,
A. M. Green.	James Needham,	Rev. Elisha Weaver,	Thomas J. Bowers.	Morris Hall,
J. W. Page.	Ebenezer Black,	David B. Bowser,	J. C. White, Jr.,	J. P. Johnson,
L. R. Seymour,	James R. Gordon,	Henry Minton,	Rev. J. P. Campbell,	Franklin Turner,
Rev. William T. Catto,	Samuel Stewart,	Daniel Colley,	Rev. W. J. Alston,	Jesse E. Glasgow.

A Meeting in furtherance of the above named object will be held

And will be Addressed by

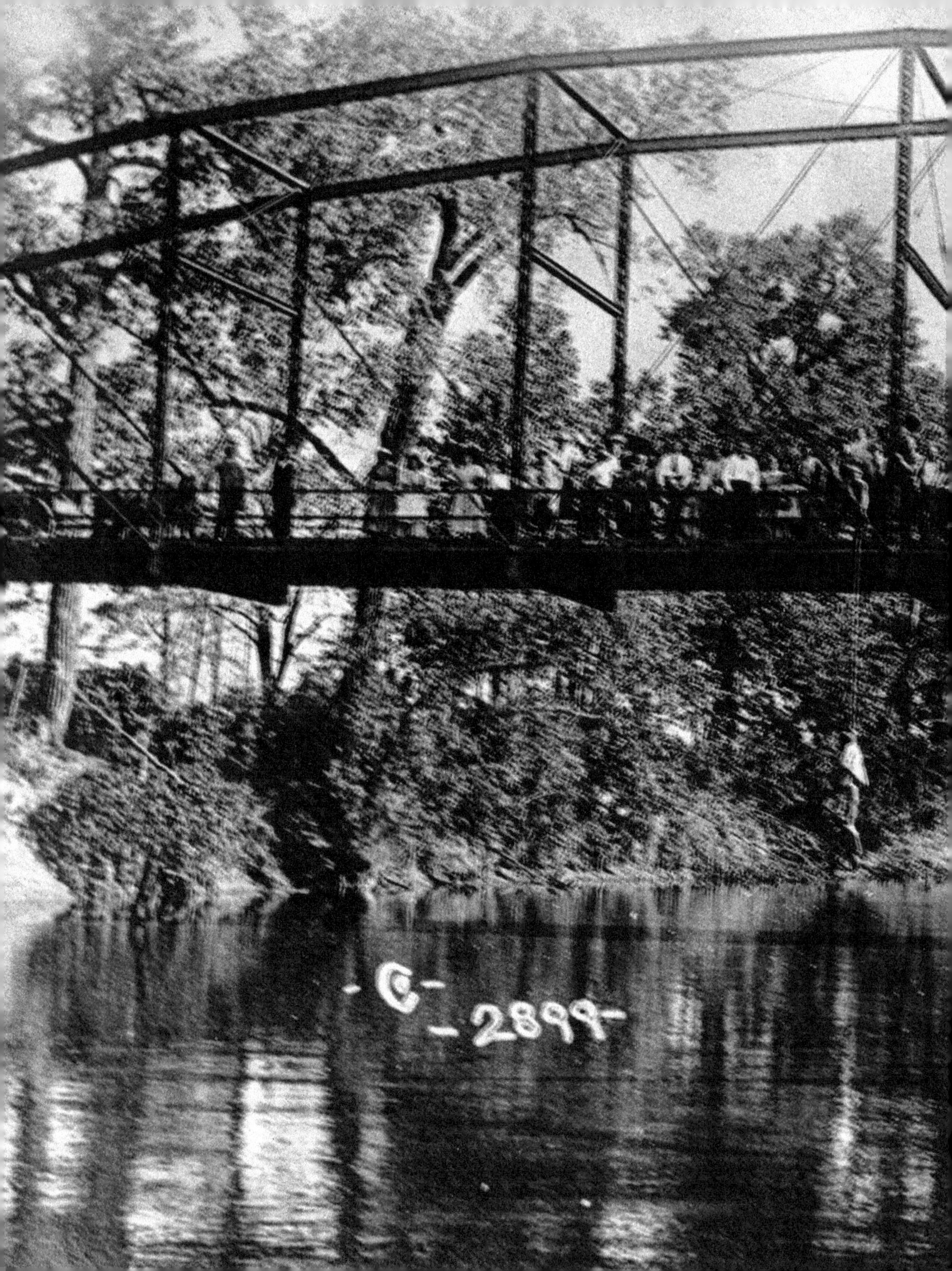
-C-
-2899-

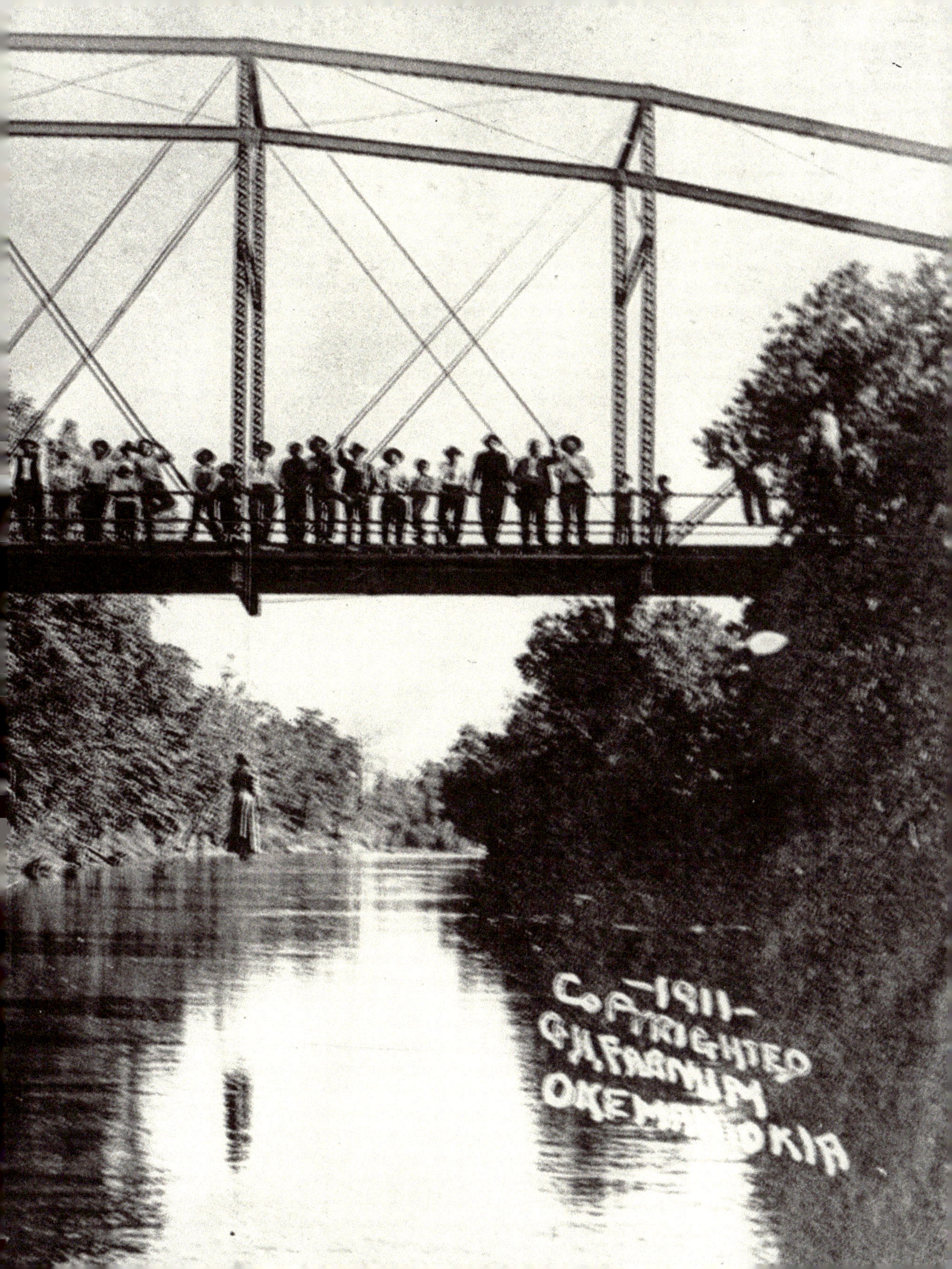

-1911-
COPYRIGHTED
G.H. FARNUM
OKEMAH OKLA

Then as now for people from disenfranchised groups who enlist the military offers a degree of dignity and security. Case in point, census data from 2018 indicates Native people have the highest national poverty rate (25.4%) and African Americans at 20.8%.[1] The U. S. Army Reserve website notes "… Historically, American Indians have the highest record of military service per capital when compared to other ethnic groups."[2]

Despite providing dignity and security living conditions were deplorable. "Soldier morale was low and desertions high. On average, the army lost fully one-fourth of its troops to desertion in the 1870s, and over a longer period, between 1867 and 1891, one-third of the army deserted."[3] Historian Louis Warren notes that "there were abundant reasons for discontent: drafty barracks, ill-fitting uniforms and boots, and a dismal diet of pork, hardtack, and coffee, which barely sustained a soldier's health. Troopers could go six months without seeing their wages, which dropped from $16/month in the Civil War to $13/month in 1871."[4] Despite this, Buffalo Soldiers had the lowest desertion rates in the army during the 1870s and 1880s, and there were zero desertions during the entire period (1875–79) that the Ninth Cavalry was stationed at Fort Garland. U. S. Colored Troops still faced discrimination during their tours of duty and many never saw their families of origin again once they joined.

What was the milieu of public messaging in the mid to late 1800s that influenced black people to participate in Manifest Destiny?

What role did print media, advertising and popular culture play in promoting and perpetuating the concept of the Western Frontier, Manifest Destiny, and ascendant civilization? An unlikely source for insight into this period can be found in a case study of the life and times of Buffalo Bill who was a master showman and an exemplar of self-promotion through print media and wheat pasted broadside advertising. His rise to fame coincided with the evolution of large-scale printing techniques.

Born William Frederick Cody in 1846 Cody was a Union soldier in the Civil War, became an Army scout participating in the Indian Wars, bison hunter and showman. Cody received the nickname "Buffalo Bill" after the American Civil War, when he had a contract to supply Kansas Pacific Railroad workers with bison meat.[5] Cody is purported to have killed 4,282 bison in eighteen months between 1867 and 1868.[6] His experience as a bison hunter led to Cody being contracted by wealthy, east coast-based businesspeople to head bison hunting expeditions for sport on the frontier.

 buffalo soldiers: reVision

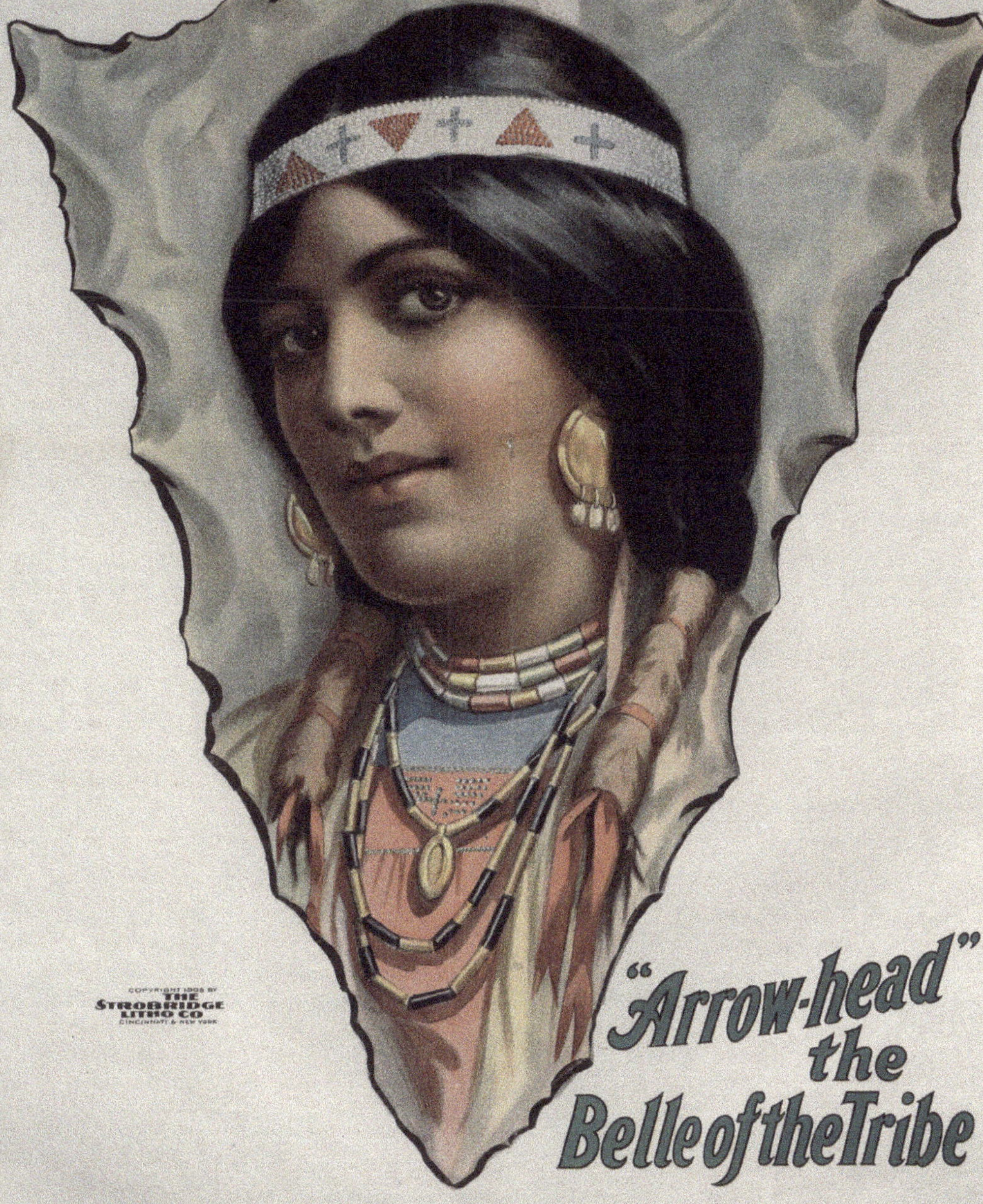

BUFFALO
WILD
BILL'S
WEST
COPYRIGHT 1908 BY
THE
STROBRIDGE
LITHO CO
CINCINNATI & NEW YORK
"Arrow-head"
the
Belle of the Tribe

Writer and historian Louis S. Warren notes that "In August 1868, Cody served as guide and hunter to the U. S. Tenth Cavalry, a segregated black unit, and his white commanding officer reported that Cody gets $60 per month and a splendid mule to ride and is one of the most contented and happy men I've ever met."[7]

In 1869, at age 23, Cody met writer, editor and playwright Ned Buntline who published his first dime novel about the life and times of William Cody on the prairie titled *Buffalo Bill, the King of the Border Men.*

In December of 1872, Buntline wrote a play for Cody titled *Scouts of the Prairie,* in which Cody starred with no previous acting experience. The show opened in Chicago and though panned by critics it had sell-out crowds from a predominantly working-class audience. This began his career as a showman in which he performed in the theater for 11 years. Seeking a more cultured audience and to distinguish himself from similar plays about the Western Frontier, Cody founded *Buffalo Bill's Wild West*, a circus-like attraction that toured annually starting in 1883 until his death in 1917.

Warren writes, "The convergence of the railroad circus with William Cody's Plains career was no accident. Circuses were widespread in American life and culture throughout the nineteenth century, but railroad expansion, the rise of corporate investment, and a revolution in print advertising—especially poster production—made for a renaissance of circuses after the Civil War."[8] Warren also notes that "Cody's rise to fame was partly a function of the changing mass press. He arrived in the popular eye as newspaper editors hit on the technique of manufacturing news rather than merely reporting it."[9]

Touring both the U. S. on the nascent transcontinental railroad system and Europe with a troupe of Native performers including Sitting Bull and 20 of his braves, Pawnee and Lakota scouts, Wild Bill Hickok, cowboys, members of the military, sharp-shooter Annie Oakley, members of horse based tribes from around the world and a herd of bison. With dozens of supporting cast members Buffalo Bill's Wild West helped define the lingering perception of the Western Frontier and Manifest Destiny through the show itself and its advertising.

Performers re-enacted the riding of the Pony Express, Native attacks on wagon trains, and stagecoach robberies. The show was said to end with a re-enactment Custer's Last Stand, in which Cody portrayed General Custer. Prior to Custer's death at Little Big Horn, the finale was typically a portrayal of

NOW IN CAMP AT READVILLE!

54th REGIMENT!

MASS. VOLUNTEERS, composed of men of

AFRICAN DESCENT

Col. ROBERT G. SHAW.

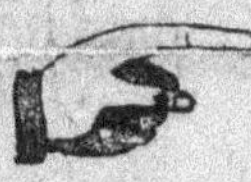

Colored Men, Rally 'Round the Flag of Freedom!

BOUNTY $100!

AT THE EXPIRATION OF THE TERM OF SERVICE.

Pay, $13 a Month!

Good Food & Clothing!

State Aid to Families!

RECRUITING OFFICE,

COR. CAMBRIDGE & NORTH RUSSELL STS.,

BOSTON.

Lieut. J. W. M. APPLETON, Recruiting Officer.

100

COLORED MEN

WANTED,

FOR NON-COMMISSIONED

OFFICERS & CLERKS

FOR UNITED STATES COLORED REGIMENTS, ORGANIZING IN THE SOUTH-WEST.

These Men are Enlisted under **SPECIAL AUTHORITY** from the War Department—must be able to Read and Write Fluently, and must be Men of Intelligence.

THEY WILL RECEIVE ALL THE

LOCAL AND GOVERNMENT BOUNTIES

AND WILL RECEIVE FROM

18 to 26 DOLLARS PER MONTH PAY,

With a Clothing Allowance of $3.50 per Month.

As the Number to be Enlisted is Limited, an Early Application will be Necessary to Ensure Acceptance.

Young Men desiring to Enlist must be accepted by the undersigned before being Mustered.

LOUIS WAGNER,

Lieut. Col. 88th Pa. Vols.,
Comd'g Camp William Penn.

TO COLORED MEN.

54th REGIMENT!

MASSACHUSETTS VOLUNTEERS,

OF

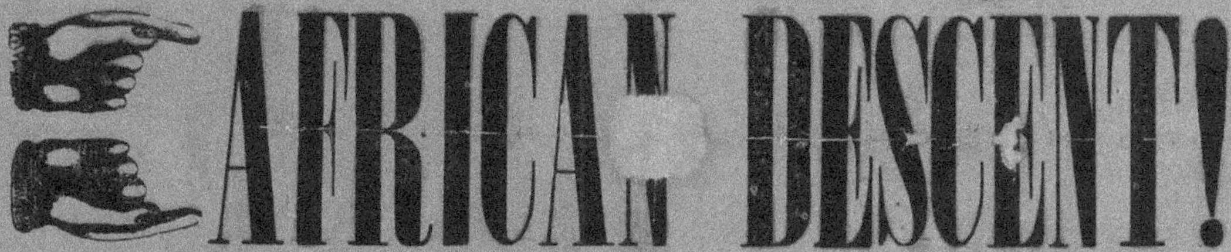

$100 BOUNTY!

At the expiration of the term of service.

PAY, $13 A MONTH!

AND

STATE AID TO FAMILIES.

RECRUITING OFFICE,

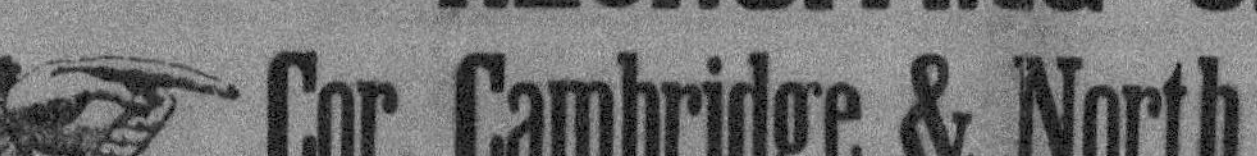

Cor. Cambridge & North Russell Sts., Boston.

Lieut. J. W. M. APPLETON, Recruiting Officer.

J. E. FARWELL & Co., Steam Job Printers, No. 37 Congress Street, Boston.

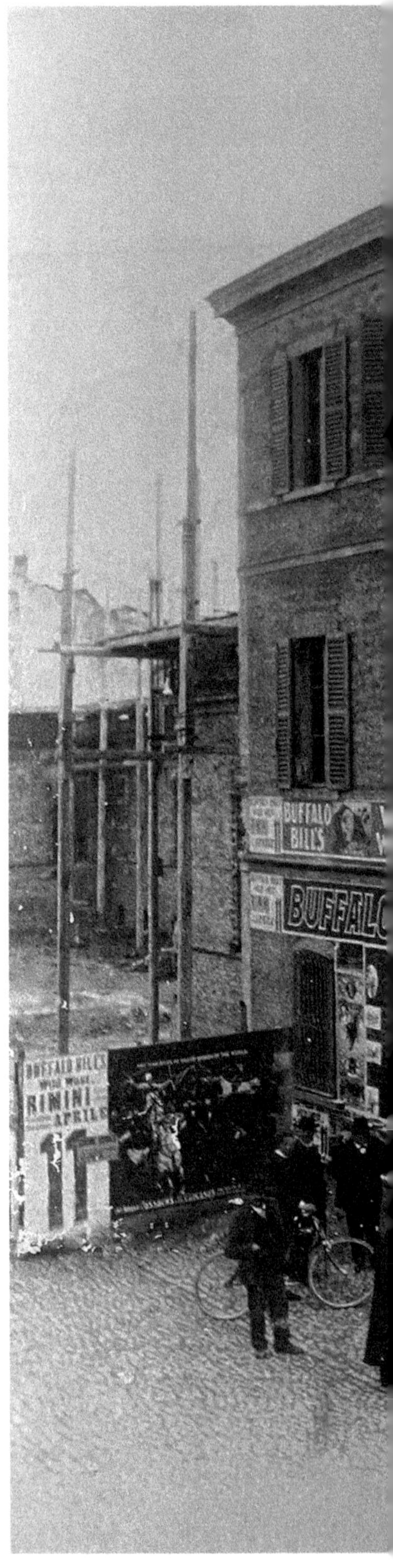

Italian building with Buffalo Bill's Wild West poster displays wrapping around the first floor exterior, ca. 1906. BUFFALO BILL MUSEUM AND GRAVE, GOLDEN, COLORADO, OBJECT ID #302

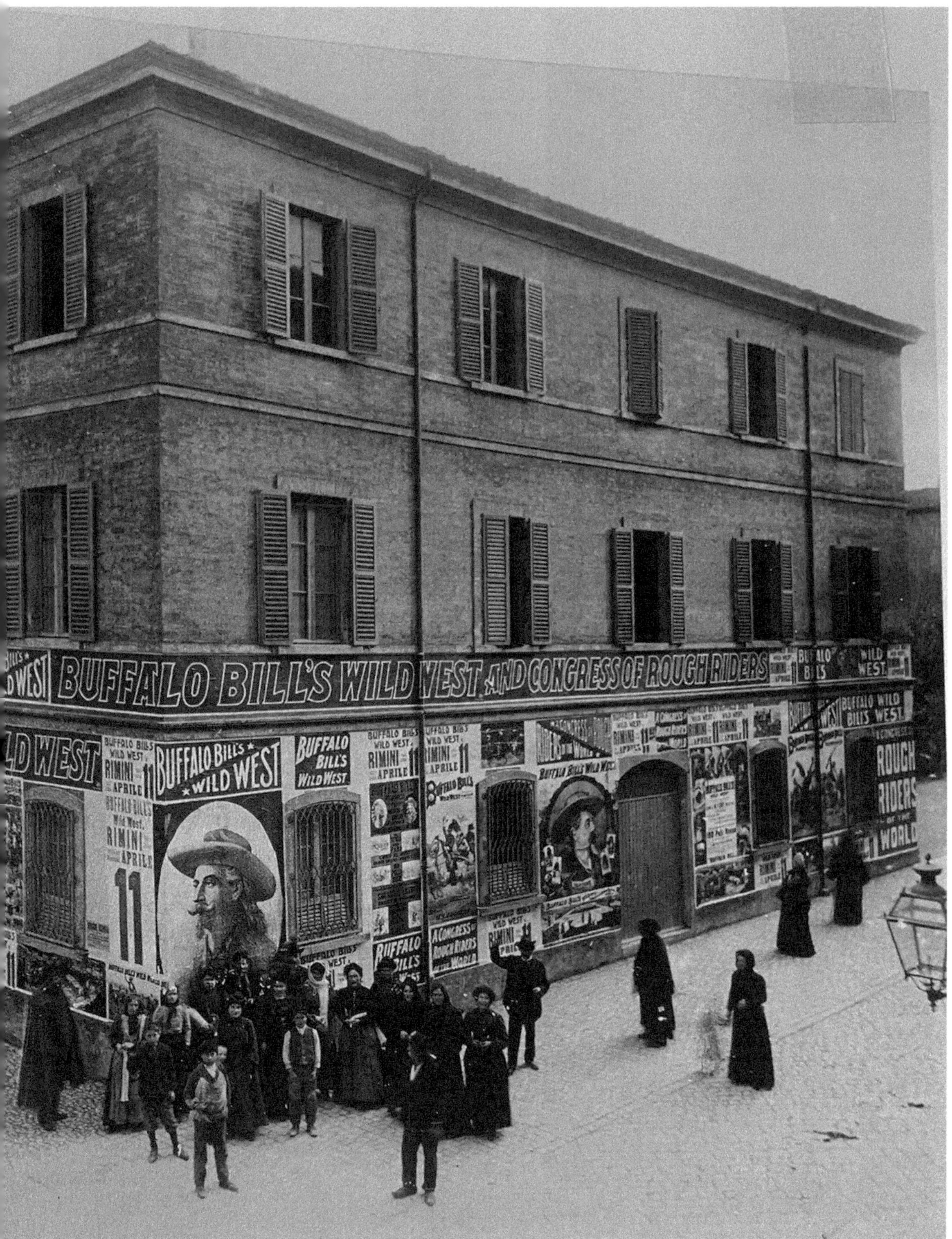

BUFFALO BILL'S WILD WEST AND CONGRESS OF ROUGH RIDERS
WILD WEST
BUFFALO BILL'S WILD WEST
BUFFALO BILL'S WILD WEST
RIMINI APRILE 11
BUFFALO BILL'S WILD WEST
BUFFALO BILL'S WILD WEST
RIMINI APRILE 11
ROUGH RIDERS OF THE WORLD
A CONGRESS OF ROUGH RIDERS OF THE WORLD
RIMINI APRILE 11

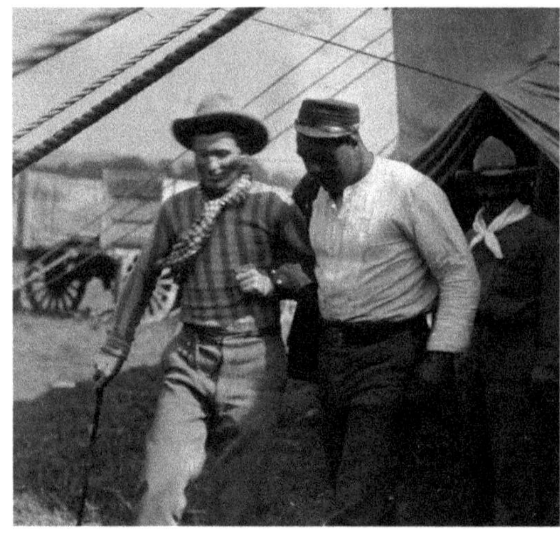

Unidentified Buffalo Soldier and cowboys emerging from Wild West show tent, ca. 1900.
MCCRACKEN RESEARCH LIBRARY, BUFFALO BILL CENTER OF THE WEST

an Indian attack on a settler's cabin. Cody would ride in with an entourage of cowboys and the military to defend a settler and his family.

Cody, like many heroes of the frontier, including Paul Bunyan, Davy Crockett, Custer, and Wild Bill Hickok, was known to take artistic license in the retelling of adventures on the frontier. It was left to the audience hearing these tales to determine truth from fiction. Writer and historian Louis S. Warren notes:

> "… The mythology of progress which western events seemed to validate, the clearly visible ascent of civilization, was easily incorporated into melodramas of frontier heroes restoring virtuous women to domestic bliss—which, in the working of melodrama, was the heart of civilization itself. Melodrama idealized domesticity. In play after play, the melodrama reinscribed the notion that personal happiness, democracy, the future of the republic, and just about every other desirable condition depended on domestic contentment, which in turn depended on chaste marriage, and of course, the "true" and unstained woman. Just as the triumph of civilization over savagery was understood as the triumph of domestic order, the salvation of the settler's cabin, so the melodrama's core plot was the rescue of the virtuous woman and her restoration to the home. Thus, audiences projected melodramatic fantasies onto Hickok, Cody and Omohundro even before they saw their plays, envisioned them saving white women from Indians even before they 'saw' them do just that on the stage."[10]

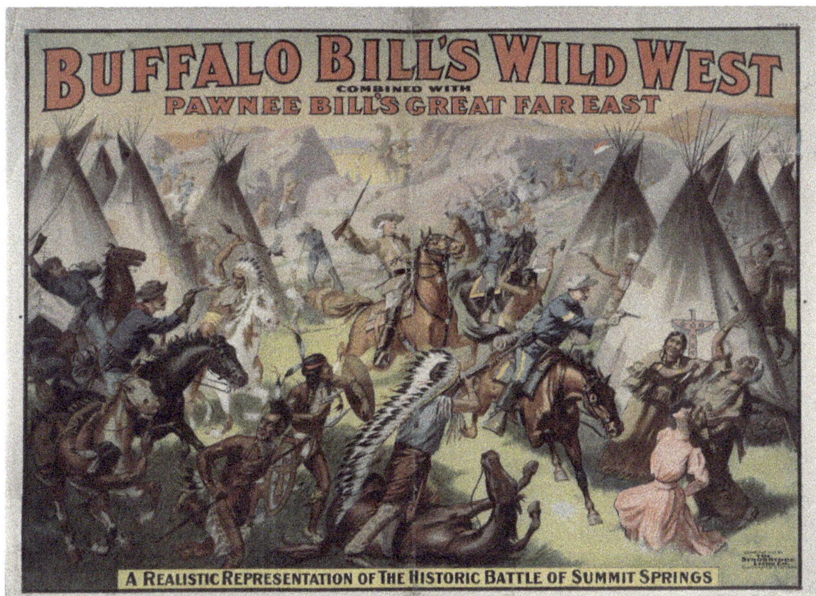

The Strobridge Lithographing Company, *Buffalo Bill & Pawnee Bill: Battle of Summit Springs*, Ink on paper, 28.5 x 38.5", 1907. COLLECTION OF THE JOHN AND MABLE RINGLING MUSEUM OF ART, TIBBALS COLLECTION

Warren continues "…The frontier's centrality to American ideas of history and progress provided not just a theory of American development, but a powerful story about how people behave and how events unfold. The advancement from primitive hunting to modern commerce, from savage disorder to enlightened civilization provided a ready-made narrative, a backstory, to every drama set there."[11] ❋

ENDNOTES

1. https://rb.gy/vcpkx
2. https://rb.gy/l71f5
3. *Buffalo Bill's America: William Cody and the Wild West Show*, Louis S. Warren 2005, page 96
4. Ibid. pp 96–97
5. Crossen, Forest (1968). *Western Yesterdays*, vol. 6, Thomas Fitzpatrick, Railroadman, Paddock Publishing.
6. Cody, William F. (1904). *The Adventures of Buffalo Bill Cody*. 1st ed. p. viii. New York and London: Harper & Brothers.
7. *Buffalo Bill's America: William Cody and the Wild West Show*, Louis S. Warren 2005, p 82.
8. Ibid. p 206.
9. Ibid. p 158.
10. Ibid. p 175.
11. Ibid. p 177.

race and

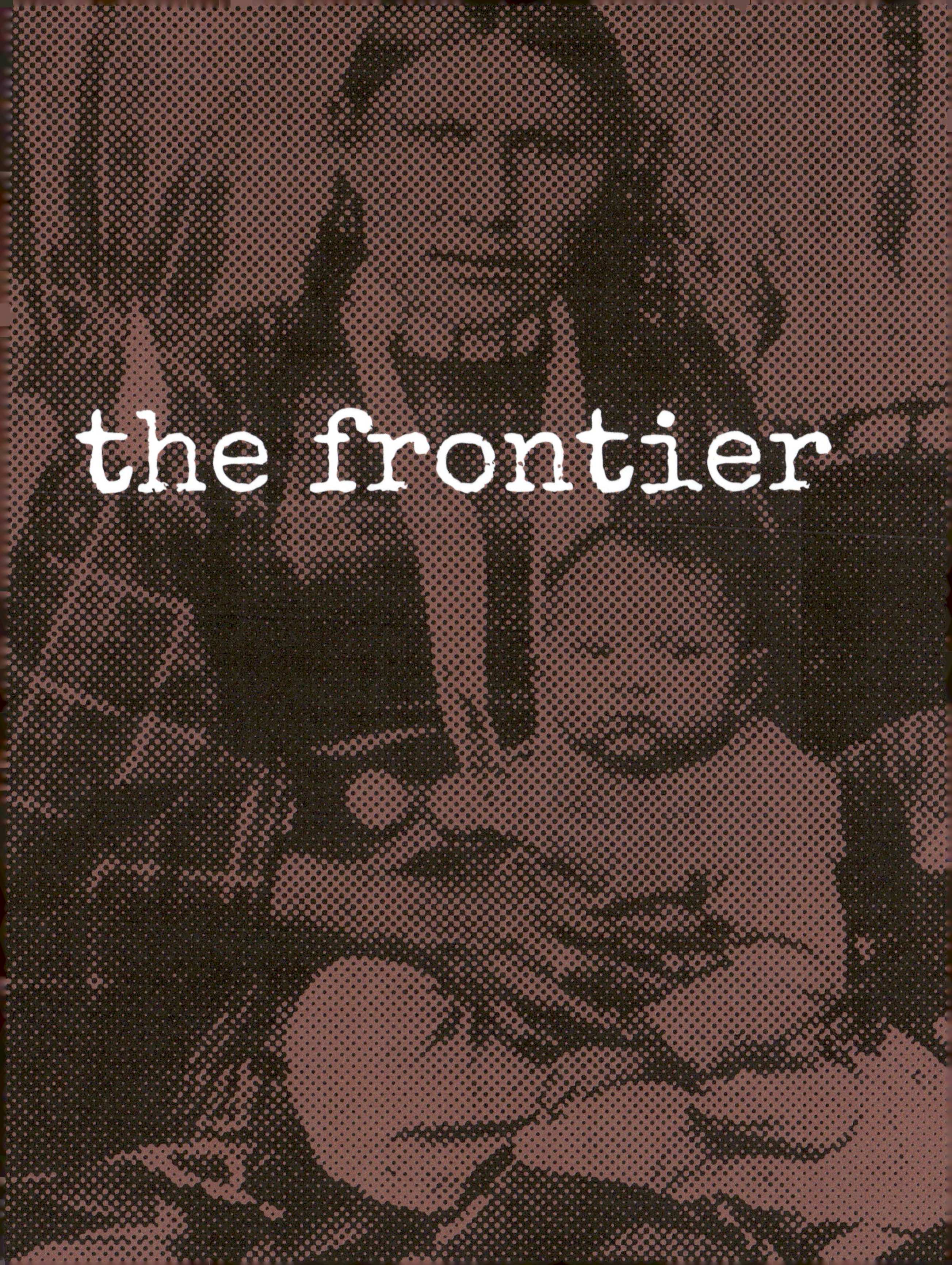

the frontier

Chip Thomas

In the introduction to his master's thesis titled *JOHN TAYLOR and Racial Formation in the Ute Borderlands 1870–1935,* historian Louis Gregory McAllister notes that the term "Western frontier" is problematic because it was constructed as a boundary between "wilderness/savagery" and "civilization." Frederic Jackson Turner, the scholar who popularized this term, saw the primary racial binary in the Southwest as being between whites and Native people to the exclusion of Mexicans, Asians and African Americans. McAllister notes that writer William Katz challenged this binary in books such as *The Black West* and *Black Indians* by centering Africans in the narrative as did historian Kenneth Wiggins Porter. McAllister writes of historian Arnoldo De Leon that he refers to the West as "a 'racial frontier' because it was a contact point where distinctly identifiable races converged."

Historian Louis S. Warren writes about this period "To most Americans, the frontier was the boundary line between the white and the red, and the army stood in defense of white homes from Indian raiders who carried white women away into savagery."[1] But racial lines weren't so distinct. While white Army personnel had reservations about the loyalty of Native and mixed-race scouts, they also admired and respected the fighting skills of their Native combatants.

Warren continues "Conditioned by generations of Indian conflict, Americans conflated the heroic Army scout and the 'white Indian,' a white man who adopted Indian woodcraft and fighting methods, combined them with a heart that remained true to the cause of civilization and contained all within a white, civilized body. If Indians embodied Nature and Europeans embodied Culture, the white Indian embodied the proper, virtuous mixing of both. He was the essence of American identity."[2] Men such as Paul Banyan, Davy Crockett, Kit Carson, Will Bill Hitchcock, Buffalo Bill and others were celebrated in dime novels, newspaper articles and stage plays as such mythic figures.

Historian Louis Gregory McAllister introduces another twist to the complexity of racial relationships on the frontier in examining the life of buffalo soldier John Taylor. Taylor was born to enslaved parents in Paris, Kentucky in 1841 where he too worked as an enslaved person. However, Taylor escaped and enlisted in the U.S. Colored Troops in Kentucky where he fought in the Civil War. Honorably discharged February 6, 1866, Taylor returned to Kentucky where he worked in corn and cotton fields until he reenlisted in the U.S. Colored Troops March 21, 1867 to participate in the Indian Wars. Taylor worked primarily as a translator, as he spoke Navajo, Hopi, Ute and Apache as well Spanish. He went on to become the first non-Native settler in La Plata County where Durango, Colorado is located.

In his master's thesis, McAllister references a gathering of settlers who reunited once a year in the early 1900s to recount their days on the frontier in southern Colorado. Amongst them in the 1930s was John Taylor.

McAllister quotes the September 1941 edition of *The Colorado Magazine* and writes,

> At this particular reunion the first person to speak was John Taylor, a
> black man from Kentucky. Taylor was a survivor of slavery and the
> turmoil of the Civil War. He was at least 85 years old, if not older, when
> he addressed the small crowd. With poise, Mr. Taylor proudly pro-
> claimed, "Yes sir, I was the first white man to settle the Pine River
> Valley." "That's right John" was the unanimous response from a
> congregation of a dozen or more grizzled white men.
>
> Somehow in this meeting of San Juan pioneers the meaning of
> "whiteness" included an ex-slave from Kentucky. Somehow this group
> of old white men resounded in agreement to the claim that Taylor was

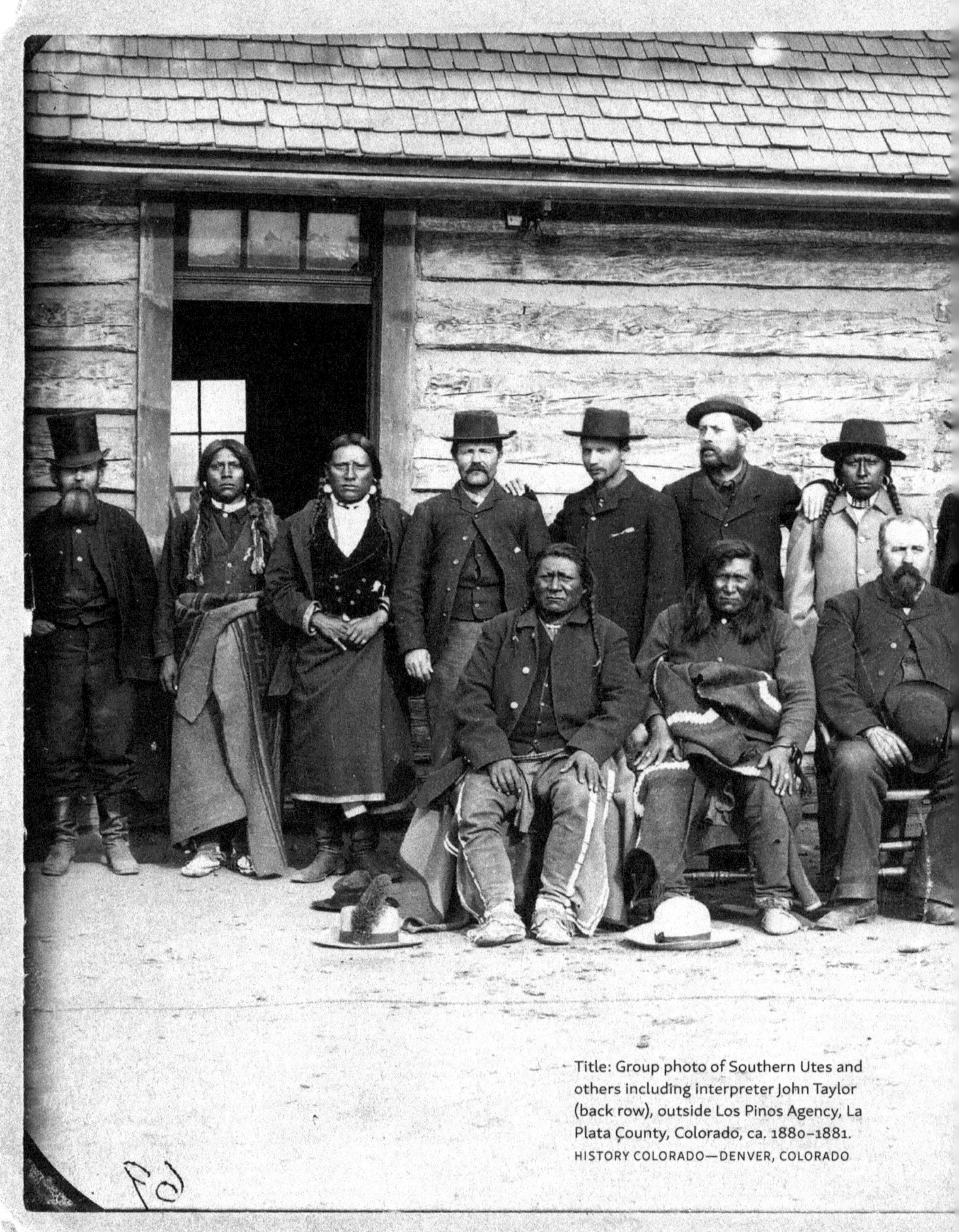

Title: Group photo of Southern Utes and others including interpreter John Taylor (back row), outside Los Pinos Agency, La Plata County, Colorado, ca. 1880–1881.
HISTORY COLORADO—DENVER, COLORADO

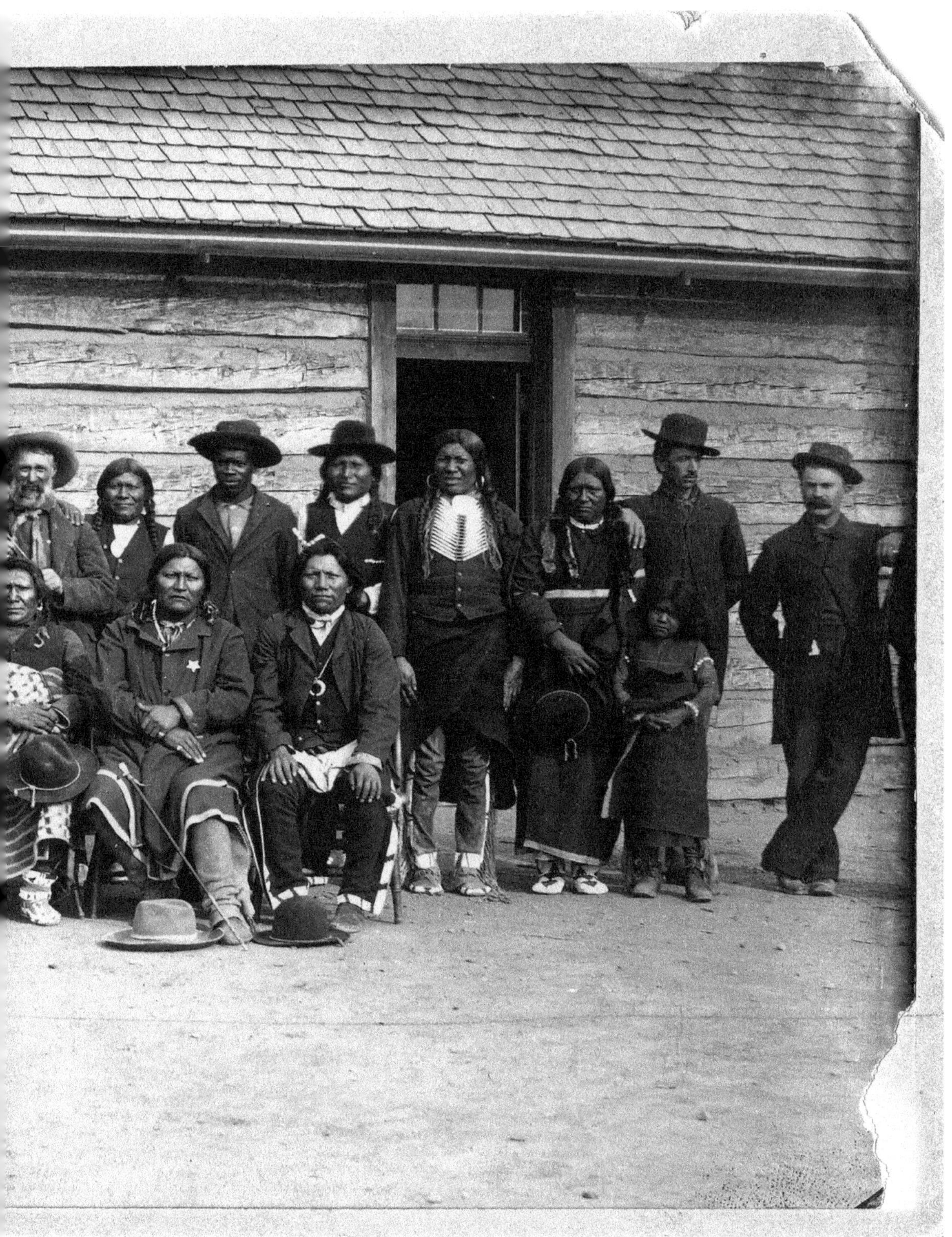

a 'white man.' Such an event clearly illustrates that Taylor's white identity transcended his skin color, ancestry or history of slavery.

McAllister writes,

> John Taylor's claim appears to contradict the common social understanding of race as it exists in the history of the United States. Taylor could not pass as white, and the racial divide created by slavery and perpetuated by Jim Crow Laws persisted long after his death in 1935. For that matter many of the old settlers attending the Pioneer Reunion most likely lived through and remembered the antebellum debate over slavery and the Civil War. Many had also experienced the War as either soldiers or civilians fighting on either side. With this common history, why was it that these Anglos were willing to support John Taylor's claim?
>
> Taylor's identity as a black white man reflects the complexity of his particular African American experience on the Ute borderlands. In this setting, Anglo settlers expressed their whiteness in relation to American Indians, Mexican Americans and Asian Americans. In fact, a number of African Americans who came out West after the Civil War noticed that the racial divide between blacks and whites was mediated by Anglo interaction with these other racialized groups in the region. Taylor's white identity was never a rejection or omission of his African American self. Taylor's whiteness was based on the dynamics of location because such an unusual claim could not persist in other sections of the country or for that matter other sections of the Southwest.

John Taylor's western experience was singular and did not represent the norm for Buffalo Soldiers. Historian Quintard Taylor reflected on the complexity of the African American and Native experience at a conference in February 2004. There he presented a paper titled "The Shifting Borders of Race and Identity: A Research and Teaching Workshop On the First Nations and African American Experience." It is Quintard Taylor's perspective on frontier racial relationships that provides a glimmer of hope and a pathway for reconciliation.

Professor Taylor writes,

> Encounters between Native people and African people in the West, the longest of any two groups of color, included an array of interactions

Dick "Buckskin" Charley and John Taylor, ca. 1904.
COURTESY DENVER PUBLIC LIBRARY

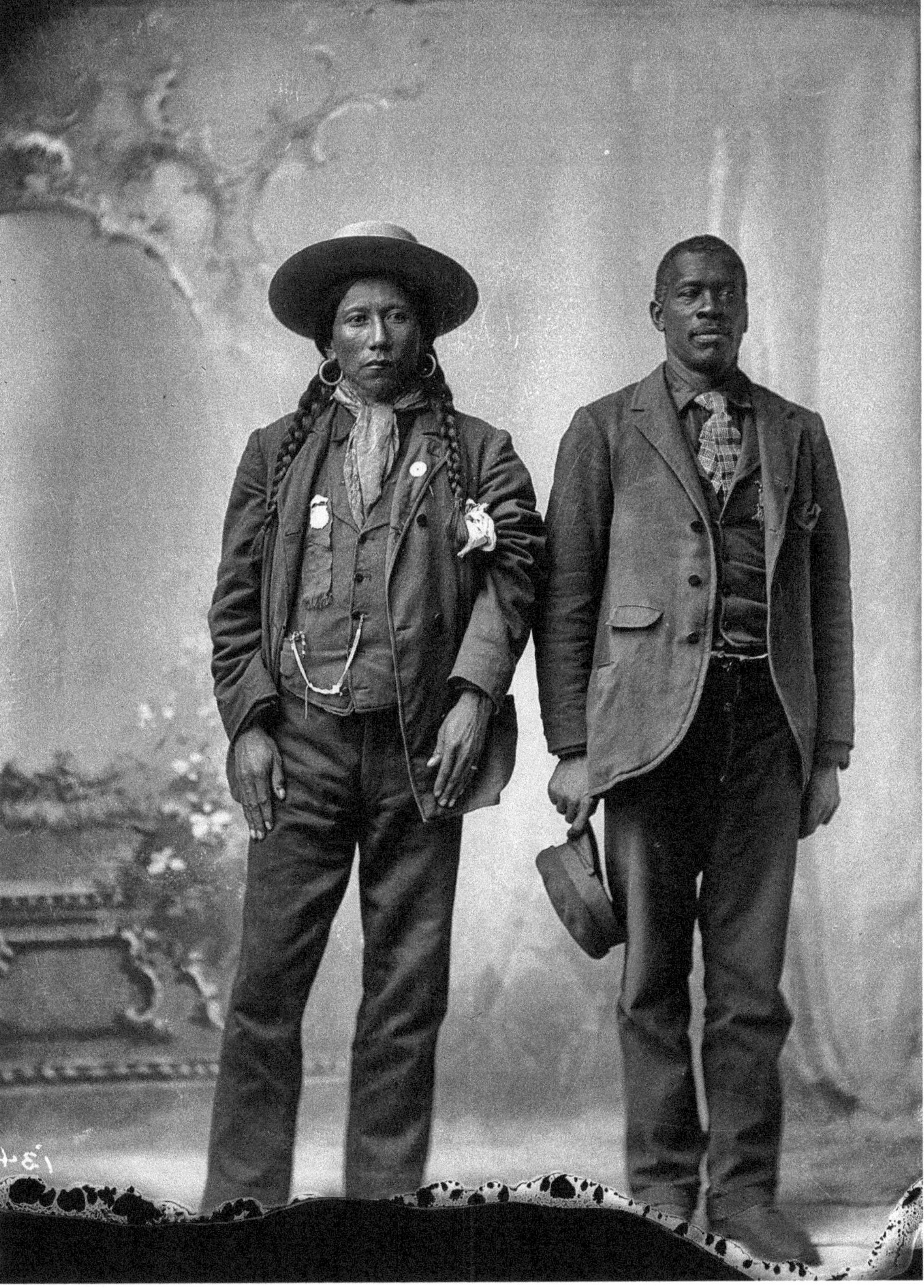

with each group in a position of power vis-à-vis the other. At various stages, Indians were victims and oppressors of African Americans. At various stages, African Americans were victims and oppressors of Native Americans. Thus, when we discuss the encounters, we must ask disturbing questions about the relationship that found expression at different times in conflict, cooperation, and accommodation.

We have an opportunity at this symposium (and beyond) to explore these relationships over time and space so that we may move beyond stereotypes about blacks and Indians that posit two equally wrong notions: namely, that the cultural divide between the races prevented any positive association, or that Indians and blacks understood their shared oppression and always struggled to defeat their common foe, the European American.

Native Americans and Buffalo Soldiers

There is no greater source of tension between Native Americans and African Americans than in the disparate recollections of the "Buffalo Soldiers," the approximately 25,000 men who served in four regiments, the Ninth and Tenth Cavalry and the Twenty-Fourth and Twenty-Fifth Infantry, between 1866 and 1900.

But as early as 1969 Native American historians, such as Jack Forbes, began to probe the moral dilemma posed by the actions of these men. Were they not instruments in the subjugation of Native peoples in a society that despised them and the Indians? In recent years Native American people and scholars have gone even farther in their critique of the black soldiers. When U. S. Postmaster General Marvin Runyon announced a "Buffalo Soldiers" commemorative stamp in 1994, representatives of the American Indian Movement (AIM) demanded both the stamp's withdrawal and a public apology. "The pain of history cannot be so easily passed over," wrote Vernon Bellecourt in *Indian Country Today*, "we remember."

Professor Taylor continues,

While it is quite clear that many contemporary Native Americans see the "celebration" of the Buffalo Soldier role in the conquest of the West as not simply wrong but offensive, the historical record is far more complex. We need to know how Native warriors felt about Buffalo Soldiers, both as soldiers and as African Americans. Presumably, they saw a distinction between black and white soldiers. Thus the name "Buffalo Soldier."

The attempt to elevate African American soldiers to heroic status on the backs of fallen indigenous warriors is wrongheaded. It is also historically inaccurate since "Indian fighting" was only a small measure of the role of black soldiers in the West. In fact, military records reveal that Buffalo Soldiers fought in proportionately fewer engagements with indigenous warriors than white soldiers. Yet, it is entirely understandable that many indigenous people hated black soldiers for carrying out orders that limited their traditional freedoms and confined them to reservations. As Native American scholar Cornell Pewewardy has aptly written, "As we retell our stories, reconstruct our history, and venture into multicultural learning we honor each other's past." To that end, both Native American and African American historians have a responsibility to learn from both sides about our mutual history. There is much work to be done regarding the reconstruction of the past of these two groups of color who have the longest history of interaction in the West, and, in fact, in the entire nation. Let us begin this work now. ✳

ENDNOTES
1. *Buffalo Bill's America: William Cody and the Wild West Show*, 2005, p. 102
2. Ibid., p. 82

ESTHER BELIN

When I approached this project—I had difficulty positioning myself in this documented narrative from approximately 145 years ago. This was the same period that my tribe was recovering from a forced march that paraded the people over 300 miles from their homeland to a prison camp at Bosque Redondo. During this time, stories of death were daily occurrences. Stories of raids and attacks targeting women for the slave market were common.

Few stories from the Buffalo Soldiers themselves exist. Piecing together a narrative of these soldiers involved many hours of reading archival records, newspapers, reference maps, and other federal legislation and Indian policy. I got unsettled and sifted. I imagined my father—an unknowing recruit for the Termination & Relocation campaign to civilize Indians—struggling in silence, silently tumbling through scenarios over and over, falling into a rhythmic meter of eliminating [Indigenous cadence and thought] & negotiating [colonial additives that pose the least harm to tribe and self]—each breaking of the silence slices the tongue [rarely changes the predetermined resolve]—the act of agency—an illusion—an erosion that numbs conscience into a smooth steady drumbeat, a fumigating linger.

And from this unsettled, sifting place, my sifting creative process began.

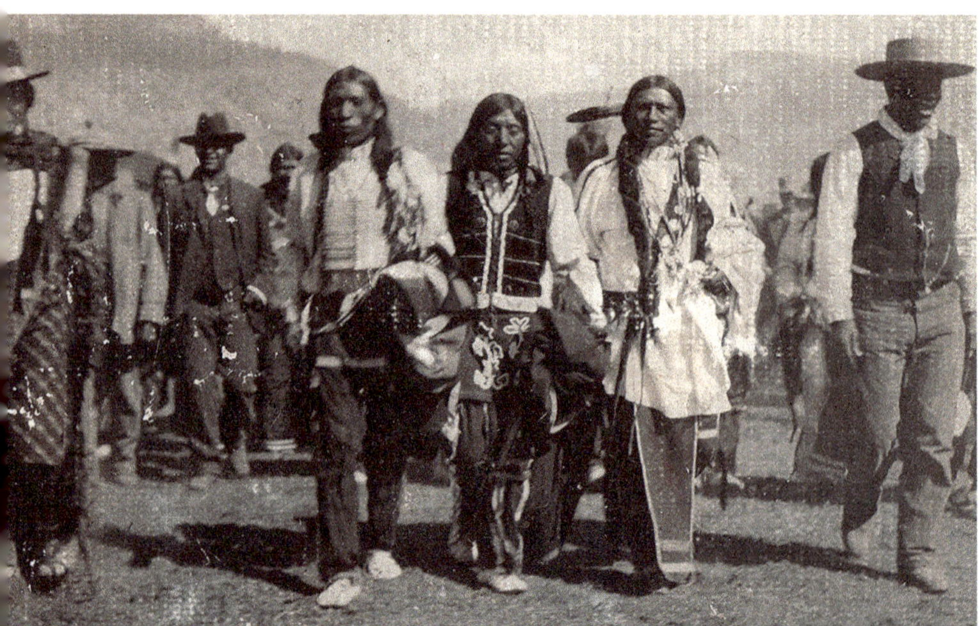

John Taylor and Native people in Durango, Colorado, ca. late 1800s
LA PLATA HISTORICAL SOCIETY

bloods bittersweet

Black & red in the borderlands

James F. Brooks

ONE

THE WOMEN, IT IS SAID, WEPT WHEN THE BLACK MAN STEPPED BETWEEN the dusty caravan of Indians who trailed in his footsteps and the charging Spanish horsemen who rode them down on the desert sands of Culiacan. He begged for their lives and freedom, and failed. He knew the slavery that awaited them, for Estevan de Dorantes had himself been enslaved in North Africa, and purchased by the Caballero Andres Dorantes. That he would become more famous than his enslaver was an accident of history.

Zunis will tell you the first white Man they ever saw was Black. Esteban de Dorantes approached the town of Halona in the autumn of 1538, scouting ahead of Fray Marcos de Niza's exploratory feeler toward the Seven Cities of Cibola. As one of only four survivors of the ill- fated Narvaez Expedition of 1527, Esteban would, unwittingly, foretell his own death by passing along the rumors of these cities, said to be clothed in gold. Although no Spaniards, trailing nearly a day's journey behind their scout, would witness what happened, Zunis may have seen their own future unravelling in the arrival of the stranger from the south. Some said he acted arrogantly, abusive toward Zuni women. Other's said he interrupted an important ceremonial. In any case, all agreed he died at Zuni hands. And yet The Black Moor lived on, even today, in the monstrous Chakwaina Katsina, who patrols the plaza dance-grounds to terrify children (and tourists) into observing proper behavior. In his death his is reborn, at once monster and cultural guardian, feared and revered in equal measure.[1]

TWO

José Lopez Naranjo, *Capitan de Guerra* and seasoned *fronterizo*, was neither Black nor white nor Indian. Yet all, as well. Born around 1670 in the troublous years that culminated in the pan-Puebloan 1680 war for independence, or the "Pueblo Revolt," his lineage had deep roots. In the region's first encounter with Spanish colonialism, Juan de Onate's entrada of 1598, Mateo, a mulatto servant of Alonso Martin Naranjo, and his Tlaxcalan wife produced a son, Domingo, who in turn formed a union with a Tewa woman from Kha'p'oe Ówîngeh (Wild Rose-Hip Village, or Santa Clara Pueblo). This also bore offspring: two sons— Lucas and José López Naranjo. Lucas became a member of the Tewa community, it seems, while José López, described as a "lobo de Indio mulatto," aligned with the Spanish blood in their lineage. The latter retreated to El Paso del Norte following the Pueblo Revolt. When don Diego de Vargas launched his *reconquista* in 1692, he served as a translator and negotiator for Vargas, ranging as far into the west as to negotiate the surrender of the Acoma rebels who had fortified Enchanted Mesa, and to take on the Zuni Pueblo of Halona as alcalde mayor. He married a Spanish woman, and acquired a land grant neighboring Santa Clara Pueblo. Yet when the Tewas of the valley joined the Tanos of the Galisteo Basin in a second desperate effort to expel the Spanish in 1696, José López aligned himself with Governor Vargas and campaigned against his kinfolk, chasing a contingent of rebels northward to their stronghold on the Mesa Prieta, where a fortuitous arquebus shot killed Lucas, among the rebel leaders. José López severed his brother's head and delivered it to the governor as evidence of his loyalty. By 1704, Vargas elevated him to Capitan de Guerra de los Indios, in command of all the Pueblo Indian auxiliaries who often made up three quarters of the Spanish campaign. The next year would see him guide the first recorded Spanish expedition north into the homelands of the "Apaches de Navajo," and return with the first of hundreds of Diné slaves that would ultimately reside in Spanish households.

Kitty Cloud (standing), with her daughter with John Taylor, Euterpe Taylor (in front of her mom). Kitty's sister is seated with her child. Circa 1904. COURTESY DENVER PUBLIC LIBRARY.

buffalo soldiers: reVision

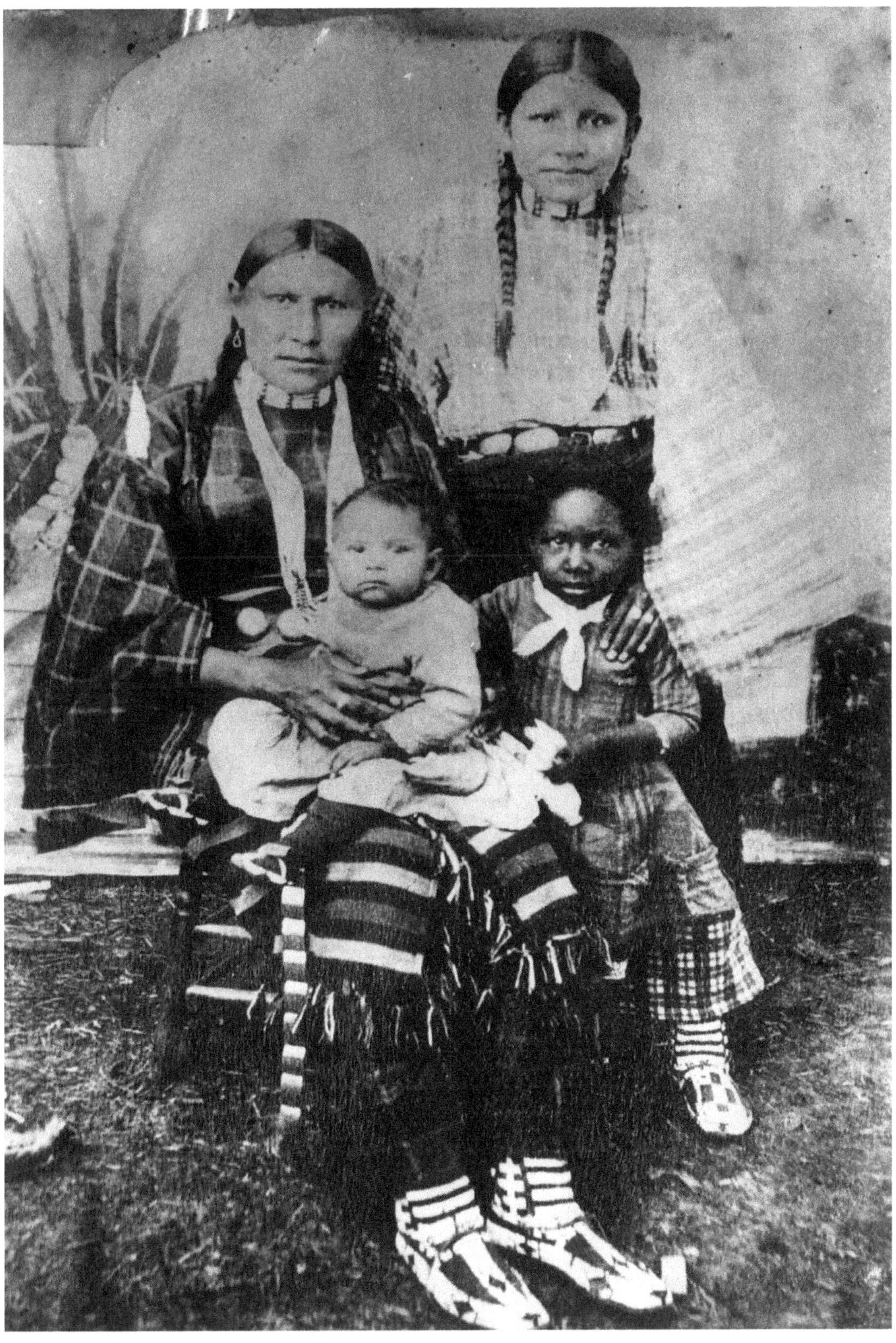

In 1720, however, as Capitan de Guerra under Governor Villasur, he led his men to destruction at the hands of Pawnees on the Loup River of today's Nebraska. He would lie among the dead; and yet the Tewa Naranjo story continues. From Tito Naranjo (b. 1938), who long taught Native American Studies at New Mexico Highlands and the University of New Mexico, to Tewa anthropologist and language activist Tessie Naranjo and her architect sister, Rina Swentzell, to Rina's daughter Roxanne, an internationally renowned artist and environmental activist, and her artist aunt Nora Naranjo-Morse, to Roxanne's children Rose B. Simpson (artist) and Porter Swentzell (educator), the lineage seems always at the forefront of the Pueblo politics, creative arts and education. In painful irony, some of these descendants fall under the exclusionary findings of the 1978 Supreme Court case Santa Clara v. Martinez, which denies tribal membership to children born to female tribal members who married outside of the tribe.[2]

THREE

Not many men in the Rocky Mountain West could claim a nobleman in their lineage. Jim Beckwourth did. His father, Sir Jennings Beckwith, impregnated his mother, an enslaved woman known as Miss Kill, on cotton Plantation, perhaps in Fredericksburg, Virginia, or near St. Charles, Missouri, sometime in the turn of the 18th century (birth years for Beckwourth range from 1798 to 1808). Uncertainty is the essence of the mercurial Beckwourth, and yet his presence is felt in memory and myth throughout the Indian West. We know that as the St. Louis to Santa Fe trade opened in the 1820s, Beckwourth was among the first men to venture into the emerging fur trade networks along the front range of the Rocky Mountains. Bold in action and verbose in recounting his adventures, he was one of the trappers who worked for the legendary company established by General William Ashley. By 1827, he was reported travelling as kinsman with a band of Crow (Absaroka) Indians who hunted Colorado's South Park for elk, deer, and market beaver. He had married Pine Leaf, a legendary Crow warrior woman, yet would in his restlessness venture far to find excitement, even to join in the U. S. Army invasion of the Seminole's Florida strongholds in the Okeechobee swamps on December 25, 1837. Back in New Mexico, he married Louisa Sandoval in Taos, yet lit out to visit his kin among the Crows and draw his Cheyenne friends into trading Bison hides at the newly established (1842) Fort Pueblo. He had a knack for appearing to witness key historical moments; the 1847 conquest of California

buffalo soldiers: reVision

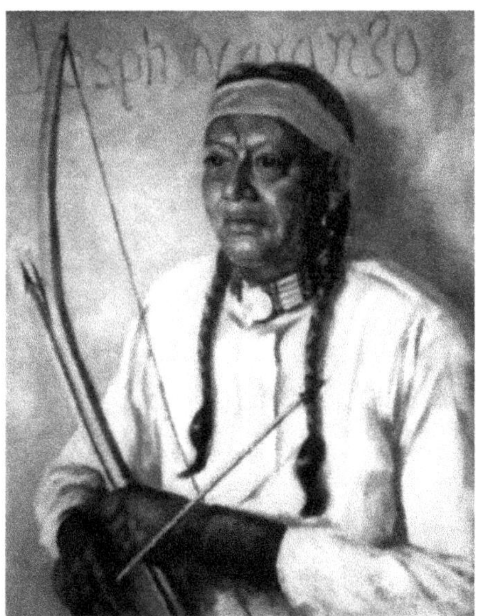

Claudine Morrow, Painting of
Jose Lopez de Naranjo, 1968.
COLLECTIONS OF THE PUEBLO
INDIAN CULTURAL CENTER

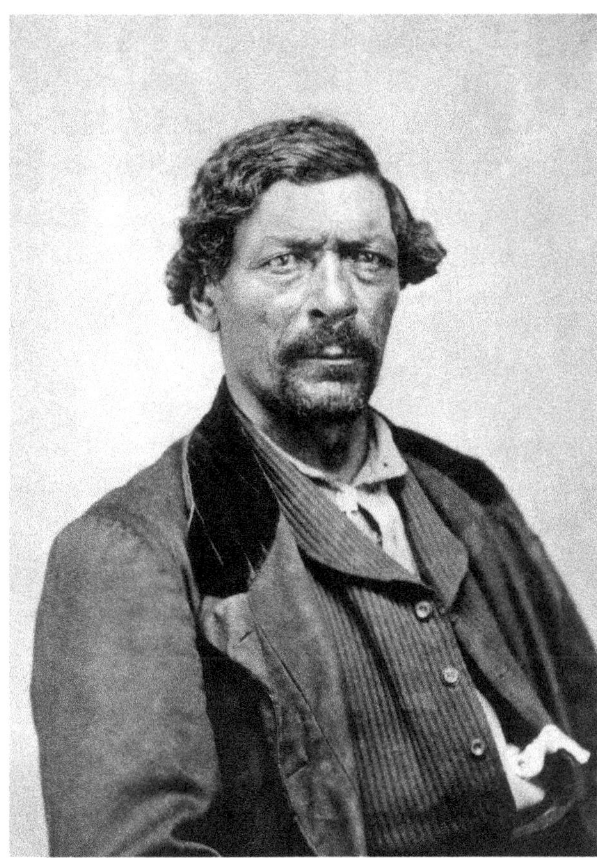

James P. Beckwourth, ca.
1860–1864. HISTORY COLORADO

among them, and seemed, no matter what the drama, to embellish the event such that he played a determinative role. And yet for all his rascality, he maintains the high regard of his Crow kinsfolk, who found in him an ally while surrounded by enemies white and Indian alike. A legend, and yet a Black man who found his way to endure as a part of the Indian story in the Borderlands.[3]

FOUR

Captain Henry Carroll and seventy-one members of the Ninth Cavalry knew they had Victorio and his breakaway band of Warm Springs Apaches cornered as they approached Hembrillo Basin from the north in the afternoon of April 6, 1880. The day before, while probing the canyons from the east, they'd encountered the old warrior's rear guard. His second in command, Lt. Conline, moved forward with 29 Buffalo Soldiers and two San Carlos Apache scouts. An intense firefight forced them to regroup and circle northward around the flanks of the

San Andres range to find an alternate path into the well-fortified Basin. Delayed, the column only entered as the sun settled behind the western ridges.

On the run since the previous September, Victorio's band of some three hundred men, women, and children, joined by several score allied Mescaleros, were hardened by years of pursuit. They wished only to be allowed to resettle at their traditional grounds around the Ojo Caliente in the Black Range of the Mimbres mountains. Even today one encounters their old campsites, trip-wired with tin-cans to alert an enemy approach. Yet the Generals in charge of Indian Policy in the Southwest wanted to concentrate and manage all Apaches, however specifically diverse, in the single reservation at San Carlos, Arizona Territory. Long standing disputes between the two groups poisoned that hope, and Victorio's people had fled to the east, expert at self-provisioning off the scattered ranchos and poblaciones of the southern Chihuahuan desert.

Carroll's D & F under Conline companies of Buffalo Soldiers numbered seventy-one men, supported by some thirty-seven Apache and Pueblo Indian scouts. Dusk fell as they entered Hembrillo Basin. Ahead lay the rocky cone of what would be called Victorio Peak; to their left, gray limestone plates thrust upward toward a ragged ridge. Apache rifle fire from stone breastworks along the ridge drove the men to dismount and scramble to benchland opposite the gunfire. Every fourth man held the horses, while the remain soldiers knelt and formed a skirmish line facing the Apaches, who numbered some 150 fighters. Throughout the night, the Apache and Pueblo scouts risked their lives to scramble into the dark canyon below to a spring that supplied the only water in that reach of the basin. The soldiers and Indians exchanged fire until dawn; the Buffalo soldiers suffering seven wounded and the loss of four horses. Conline himself suffered four wounds. Late for lack of water for his own troops, Captain Carroll arrived in the basin on the 7th, with additional troops and Apache scouts. Sensing the change in battlefield advantage, Victorio set a rear guard that allowed the two or three hundred women and children among his Warm Springs and Mescalero Apache followers to retreat to the south, and ultimately, across the border to Mexico. On October 15, Victorio and the remainders of his fugitive band would be trapped and destroyed by Mexican Army regulars at Tres Castillos.[4]

Ironically, Colonel McLellan, commanding officer of the (white) 6th Cavalry, which arrived at dawn the next morning, would author the incident report for the engagement. McLellan disparaged the Black 9th Cavalry as unprepared, sick from bad water, and lacking in initiative, and crediting his own units as their saviors, as well as the threat that forced the Chiricahuas to disengage. Only decades later would a compilation of regimental monthly returns by George Hamilton, who rose to be a Captain in the 9th, make clear the conditions under which the USCT men had maintained composure and discipline with minimal losses. ✹

ENDNOTES

1. For the story of Esteban, and Indian-African relations in Northern New Spain, see Dedra McDonald, "Intimacy & Empire: Indian-African Interaction in Colonial New Mexico, 1500-1800, in Brooks, *Confounding the Color Line: the Indian African Experience in North America* (University of Nebraska Press, 2001).

2. Naranjo is a cloudy figure in the documents, with various racial designations (lobo, mulatto, coyote) but clearly rose to a privileged place in the Spanish colony with his linguistic and martial skills. See biographical sketch in *The Navajos in 1705: Roque de Madrid's Campaign Journal*, edited, translated, and annotated by Rick Hendricks and John P. Wilson (Albuquerque: University of New Mexico Press 1996) 118–120; for his role in suppressing the Pueblo Revolt, see Frances Leon Swadesh, "The Structure of Hispanic-Indian Relations in New Mexico." In *The Survival of Spanish American Villages*, edited by Paul Kutsche, 53–62. Colorado College Studies, no. 15. Colorado Springs: Colorado College, Research Committee.

3. NPS Historian William Gwaltney has written a survey of sources and stories on Black men in the fur trade…http://lestweforget.hamptonu.edu/page.cfm?uui d=9FEC4006-CDFF-44A2-E3D69CC34C3AE4FE; for Beckwourth lineage, see: https://www.pueblolibrary.org/Beckwourth; for his adventures, see https://www.beckwourth.org/Biography/crow.html.

4. Karl W. Laumbach, "Fire Fight at Hembrillo Basin," , *Archaeology*, Vol. 54, No. 6 (November/December 2001), 34–39.

family and k'é

Sunny Dooley

MY FATHER'S MOTHER, *NANIIBAH*, WAS A TALL, ELEGANT WOMAN. SHE was a kind and hospitable lady who always provided a feast of lamb when we came to visit her. She was soft spoken, always shared a smile with a twinkle in her eye when she talked about me with my mom, while I sat with them. She wanted me to hear what she said about me.

On the way home, as I sat on the tire hump in the back of the pick-up truck, I would relish the compliments she said and smile.

She was one of the strong women mentors who came to my *kinaaldá* coming-of-age ceremony. Her quiet strength reinforced her teachings to seep deeply into my understanding of what it would take to become the young lady that would carry forth the matriarchal teachings handed down from all the women before her. She knew those teachings would root in me. She emphasized the importance of *k'é*—a concept of shared kindness interwoven with gratitude and respect all at once: this value binds our families with a deep abiding friendship of love and care.

"Always speak with k'é. Express k'é always. Do not be without k'é. K'é is a stronghold." She was straight forward and honest with these teachings. She lived it.

Visiting her several years later, she told me the story of her clan, *Naasht'ezhi Tábąąhá* Diné. She said the Tábąąhá Diné lived near the Naasht'ezhi/Zuni people. As time went on the Zuni were attacked by a group of foreigners coming from lands not found around here. What they were doing here, what they were looking for could not be understood. These people were incredibility aggressive and eventually attack the village. They took a number of women and raped them. The woman who survived this violence did not return to the village. These roaming women were accepted and welcomed into the nomadic clan of

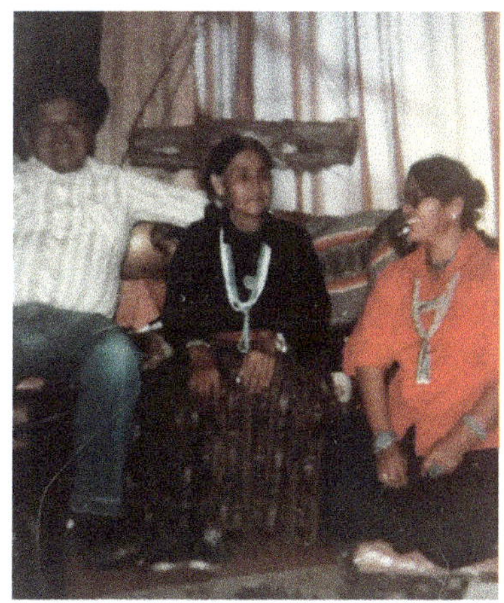

Sunny Dooley with her mother and father. COURTESY OF THE AUTHOR

the Tábąąhá. When these women birth their babies, they became the clan group Naasht'ezhi Tábąąhá Diné.

The words she said were: *Ana'i* (foreigner) *biyi'* (belong) *naa t'ezh* (raped near Zuni). The word *t'ezh* also indicated being blackened. I never could completely understand if the babies birthed were darker skinned. She recommended when I was introducing myself with my clans, I should just mention the abbreviated clan name of Tábąąhá (By Water's Edge) Diné. She mentioned it would be more easily accepted, and that saying the longer clan name may cause discomfort among certain clan groups. This story caused a curiosity in me.

It is known that among the foreigners that invaded and pillaged the village of Hawikuh, near present day Zuni, New Mexico, there was a man that included the Moorish slave: "Estevanico first appears as a slave in Portuguese records in Morocco, with him being sold to a Spanish nobleman in about 1521. In 1527 he joined the Spanish Narváez expedition to explore "La Florida," present-day Northern Mexico and Southern United States."[1]

He has been referred to as "the first great African man in America."[2] He became a folk hero in the folklore of Spain and legend in New Spain, his exploration and cataloging of the Gulf of Mexico, and what is today modern Florida and Texas, resulted in numerous legends about him.[3,4] During his final exploration and disappearance in New Mexico, and what would become the Southwestern United States, he became mythologized as part of stories involving the Seven Cities of Gold in Santa Fe de Nuevo México.[5]

Was my *Nalii* (paternal grandmother) Naniibah's (She Who Journied Back from War) ancestors one of women descendants raped by Estevanico?

Is this the reason why she emphasized the importance of maintaining k'é as a pivotal family value to be perpetuated?

My Nalii Naniibah's ancestry persevered because they were shown a great abundance of k'é. Her namesake carried down through the proceeding generations indicated the characteristics of coming through turmoil and reestablishing a life of vitality. She made living k'é a fundamental value of living a life of *Hózhó*: holding blessed and unblessed events in equal understanding. I understand this:

Tódik'ǫzhi nishłį Naasht'ezhi Tábaahá Diné báshíchchíín. Taachnii doo Kinyaa'áanii dashicheii. Tsé nahabiłnii 'éí dashicheii. Ákót'éego diné asdzáán nishłį.

I am Salty Water Clan. I am born of the Zuni People adopted by the Water's Edge. My matriarchal grandfather is Red Forehead People. Upon the death of my grandfather, my grandmother's new husband adopted her children. He is Towering House People, my patrilineal grandfather is the Rock Fortress People, are my nalii. These clans are my relatives.

By knowing where I come from, I know k'é. I know it is a value that is necessary to survive. I also know that by knowing naming all my clan affiliations, I am establishing the eternal manifestations of ancestral knowledge that tells generational stories of perseverance woven in k'é. I consistently re-establish who my relatives are. It makes it difficult for me to be disrespectful to anyone I meet.

If in my ancestral genealogy there is African Moroccan DNA, there should not be any prejudiced expressed towards the Diné people who are born of African ancestry. As Diné people, we all have k'é as a fundamental value. We share it with one another on every occasion we greet one another. K'é is our breath. My Nalii Naniibah's teaching is crucial: k'é is essential to survival. ✸

ENDNOTES

1. en.wikipedia.org/wiki/Estevanico
2. Herrick, Dennis. *Esteban: The African Slave Who Explored America*. Albuquerque: University of New Mexico Press, 2018. ISBN 9780826359827.
3. "Estevanico: The man, the myth, the legend." *Our Weekly*, Los Angeles. February 15, 2019, retrieved September 6, 2022.
4. "Estevanico." Texas State Historical Association website. July 19, 2016, retrieved September 6, 2022. tshaonline.org/handbook/entries/estevanico
5. "Mystery confines Estebanico, black explorer of U. S. Southwest". AP NEWS website. July 14, 2021, retrieved September 6, 2022.

ESTHER BELIN

Collecting interviews, reports, images, the stories about Buffalo Soldiers culminate into a trajectory about critical decisions—about the humanity, genetics, environment of these lives unfolding into a high desert plain tethered down with political border lines, governmental legislation crashing into/scrambling over (smudging chalk lines) of empire history—Indigenous, colonial, genocidal—

The ephemera, the digital, the auditory and visual—become monuments—weight-laden masses—sometimes demanding attention—

Do I take on the role of mad scientist scheming to understand the chemistry of systemic racism or those symptomatic effects on individuals, or am I an audience of the colonial theater isolated from the genetic mutations in my DNA, leaving me voiceless, motionless, numb to the battering and protruding blunt occurrences between breath and utterances twisted in violence, emotion flattened in the white space of marginalia—visually manifested as silence, acquiescent—

What if the sharpened edges of the flattened silence slices me like a lateral paper cut—I dangle like beaded fringe adornment no one notices—on the buckskin dress ripped from the muti-lated—dead-center of the crosshairs scope on a rifle, allotment-parceled, aftermath blackened-ash ink scrawled Body—the fringe witness to the act—blood-marred in horror yet collected and enamored for its beauty and pattern and creative cleverness—

Am I the poet, the artist—attempting to find the inspired creativity to more, more, more—educate, promulgate, emancipate, highly-pressurized, frack-heated hegemony served with a slice of hot corn bread and campfire coffee—

Am I the thickly dotted agenda using hate and destruction—destroying deference with hatred from left-handed articulations dyslexified—

Am I the interpreter on staff—stuttering and fidgeting—in fear and awe—fevering off smallpox riddled rants, desperately deciphering the thunder struck land in a monsoon torrent—my mouth gaping open and paralyzed from atomic energy no longer oozing but raging into mushroom cloud explosives targeting the heart or maybe the vocal cords first—

Or am I the scholar doing the analytical, contextual close reading of the aftermath of the bomb—wearing protective gear, mindful of land mines—nuclear debris—radioactivating growth like a fetus, full-term in seven-generations—

after Etheridge Knight, Terrance Hayes

How are we all related?
If I taped everyone's picture to a wall and connected us with thread—what would I see?
              what would
        I find out?
                I would see mostly men—
               men of color . . . . . 5 shades of color absorption

If I go too far back
the butcher-sharp edge of a bayonet tries to slice between my backbone
searching for the space
between the peace & love knotted muscle,
and the "fuck you settler" half-smile

AND are the settlers really settled OR are they satiated with chicken-scratching automations
       pre-measured doses of colonial protein & Indigenous earthseed?

is that being settled?
     settlers live out their definition
     disturbing the soil with their
     species—invasive & thriving
     replicating & cloning
     pinning down bloodlines in anaerobic digesters

and there are women
               black, Indigenous, white
not yet a three-strand braid—right now—windblown, tousled hair

in this formula—am I perpetuity?
the unsettled one
allergic to the consequential conditions
of limited sovereignty

                Manifests as chronic eczema

chronic absence of air   my Flesh can no longer filter
      minute dial adjustments to the new levels
      of less-ness
divisioning (selves), a constant (re)calculation
like treaty-word slashes (now self-afflicted)
on my wrist

Yes, I know the procedure   500 years of modeling behavior [creates]

another Doctrine of Discovery rapid release capsule
more frequent, concentrated doses
        how to hygienically colonialize in 5-steps
     only 4-steps to congressionally relieve phantom pain
          & adaptations for pandemics

I am swimming far far down the ancestry line—before the slaughter, before the glittering
world. The Cicada chants, methodical soothing songs breathing life back into me.

twenty years ago and was employed as a laundress and nurse by many prominent families of the then young city. These people will be surprised to know that the faithful, respectful, modest woman was a man and is now an inmate of the insane asylum in this city, having ben sent here from the county court at Trinidad yesterday suffering from a mild mania, his delusion being that an Italian with a bear is constantly following him and trying to force him to dance with the bear for the amusement of the public.

For twenty years or more this negro man has successfully masqueraded as a woman without in any way giving rise to any suspicions as to his real sex. Except on the one subject of the bear and the Italian he is perfectly rational and is a splendid type of the deferential house servant of the ante-bellum days in the south. His only answer to a question as to why he took to wearing woman's clothes is that he just wanted to. No other reason is known. Telling of his life he says he served through the civil war and was a body servant to General Sherman and to General Grant also.

Son after the close of the war and when he had begun to wear women's clothes, he came to Pueblo and worked in half a dozen prominent families whose names he mentions. Some few years ago he went to Trinidad and as a woman was employed as a nurse and laundress and was and still is as highly regarded by every one there as in Pueblo.

Five or six months ago he gave evidence of insanity as spoken of above. He, or she as he was then known, was adjudged insane by the county court and was ordered committed to the insane asylum as Cathy Williams. There being no room for women patients at the asylum Cathy Williams was brought to this city and put in the private asylum then in existence in the Mount Pleasant house on Tenderfoot hill.

The physician in charge granted a private interview to the new patient at the patient's request. Cathy Williams then announced that "she" was a man and that "her" name was William Cathay. On account of his mental malady it was decided inadvisable then to compel Cathay to change habits of dress that had existed for twenty years and accordingly he was allowed to continue to wear dresses, and was assigned quarters apart from the other patients. Though from his dress apparently a woman Cathay seemed to have had an intense antipathy for all women and avoided them as much as possible. He was put in charge of the laundry but said nothing to the other women except to issue his instructions and he ran the department to perfection.

Finally the peculiar conditions necessitated in the care for Cathay and the demand for room for other patients, several of whom could be provided for in the quarters assigned him, decided the management of the institution, which is now located in the L. B. U. property on Victoria avenue, to notify the Las Animas county authorities to remove Cathay. He was taken back to Trinidad Sunday attired as a woman and known officially as Cathy Williams. But Cathy Williams passed out of existence in the county court there Monday when William Cathay was adjudged insane. The individual who left Pueblo as a woman Sunday came back yesterday as William Cathay, a man, and was committed to the insane asylum where he now is.

Cathay was resplendent in new clothes when he reached the city yesterday and seemed to enjoy his changed dress and the freedom from the deception which he had maintained for so many years. He is about fifty years of age, moderately stout and of medium height. Some years ago he froze his feet and amputation of the toes was necessary so that he walks in rather a halting fashion with the aid of a stick.

usher Maude Anderson, Edna Bowman, ra Ferguson, Ethel Waldron, Neill terson, Rose Stout, Jennie Thom Lillian Holden, Josephine Thom , Sarah Comstock.

THE PROGRAMME.

Miss escott's Testimonial Recital April 28.

The stimonial recital to be given Miss riade Prescott on the evening of A 28 at St. Andrew's hall, mess. prom to be a most decided success musi and financially. The program prepared for the occasion will be a lows, and a perusal of it will conv any lover of music that a rare treat n store for those who are fortuna nough to attend:

PROGRAMME.

Part First.

1. Q tette.......................
M s. Howe, Greer,
Haines and Loor
2. P solo.........................Selected
Miss Lillian Jancke.
3. V n solo, Etude Cantabile..Gotha
ittle Miss Carlotta Rice.
4. R ing.............................Selected
Miss Daisy Duggins.
5. V solo, Seventh Air....De Beriot
Miss Pearlade Prescott.
6. G Banjo solo....................Selected
Miss Cora Davis.
(Banjo duett....................Selected
M Cora Davis and Master Cecil Hart.

Part Second.

1. V duet, Now the Silver Moon
.............................George Nevin
a Comstock and Mr. Oaks.
2. Z r solo, "Sounds from Home,"
.....................................Gungel
Mr. A. F. Kinsel.
3. S no solo, Forbidden Music..
.....................................Sastolden
Mrs. Charles Sleeper.
4. V n solo...............................
An te from Mendelssohn's Concerto
Miss Prescott.
5. C ralto solo, The Fairest Vi of My Soul....................Lessen
Miss Jean Groff.
6. P solo, Regata Veneziana....Liszt
Miss Jancke.
Miss lian Jancke and Mrs. H. B. McCoy, accompanists.

T s are now on sale at Harper's Pueb Music House and the store of the hmer Jewelry Co. The Chieftain es to see St. Andrew's hall filled to i most capacity the night of the 28th.

ARDSMEN'S LAST PAY.

Pay ster Davis Will be Here This Evening.

P aster Harry T. Davis will arrive in t city this morning and will pay the mbers of the National Guard for thei rvices at Leadville. This closes up pay roll and when Colonel Davis com es his trip he will have paid eve man who did any service for the sta the Leadville campaign. The amo to be paid out here today is abo $1,500.

CUT IN THE ARM.

Sm Boys Have a Fight on East Second Street.

A e result of a scuffle last night in Eas ueblo Herb Cramer, a boy living at east Second street, is suffering fro small stab wound in his arm and Ed llins, another boy, who also lives on Second street, has a criminal cha against him. Young Collins wa rested by Officer Swan and his sto that he was coming across the str when he was accosted by Young Cra and stone throwing and hard wor ensued. Collins had an open kni his hand all the time and in the scu that followed Cramer was cut. A on dressed his wound and pronou it not dangerous.

EXCELSIOR JR.

Rice's "Excelsior Jr." a ss, which, when produced City, at Hammerstein's ter, received not only the icisms, but the approval ics of the metropolis. E. haps the best producer o sa in this country. In " he is said to have eclipse efforts in the way of scen and the various accesso for a complete production Messrs. Howe & Berry h outright from Mr. Rice th phernalia used in the New tion, which is composed o Henry Hoyt and Frank of established merit in th scenery. The company t Berry have engaged to p sior Jr." is one of the been gotten together in a tion. The principal men Sadie Martinot, Joe Ca Strickland, Johnny Pag George Ohnl, Nell McNe Strickland. In addition t chorous of forty selected cluded in this great pr have been thoroughly dr original conductor of the traction, Mr. John J. B Braham has been secur Howe and Berry, and w augmented orchestra whe presented at the Grand t your seats at the box o prices 25, 50, 75 cents, $1 a

THE NOTED PA

SPRING IS H

It Must Be So, For a Big C ing May 18.

Spring has come. Ther about it. Spring and the iably come together, and t has been in town. This cus man is the avant co show that has never exhib but which comes with a perior to anything of the in Colorado. The circus Ringling Bros.' Worlds G and the date here is Tue While Ringling Bros. are known in Pueblo, there is they will leave a reputa will henceforth give them place in the regard of l arenic amusements. Thi now exhibiting in Chicag sands of people are daily tained by what is declared est and most extensive cir le and hippodrome in th idea of the size of the gained from the fact that cars are required to tran aphernalia from city to formances are given in a drome pavilion, with sea for over 10,000 persons; th rings, two stages, an im space and a quarter-mile track; the artists number 400 horses, twenty-five ele cages of rare wild anima of unique and curious fe ling Bros.' great show wil be a revelation to Pueblo

VIA THE GREAT RO ROUTE.

living their best lives

Two Buffalo Soldiers ahead of their time yet of their time

My childhood education led me to believe that the natural course of development is towards improvement of self and society. While debate continues regarding which epoch marked the high point of humanity, individuals in each era made ways to realize their full potential. This section looks at two such unlikely examples of Buffalo Soldiers who led noteworthy lives.

cathay williams

Chip Thomas

CATHAY WILLIAMS IS CELEBRATED AS THE FIRST AND ONLY FEMALE Buffalo Soldier. Born to an enslaved mother and a free father in Independence, Missouri in 1844, she worked as a house enslaved person on the Johnson plantation on the outskirts of Jefferson City, Missouri. In 1861, at age 17, she worked for the Army as a cook and washerwoman. In 1866, Cathay Williams enlisted for a three-year tour with the 38th Infantry Regiment under the name William Cathay, presenting herself as a man despite a cursory medical examination.

Though William Cathay enlisted for 3 years, she experienced multiple hospitalizations where she was discovered to be a woman, and was honorably discharged October 14, 1868. Undeterred, she again disguised herself as a man to join the U.S. Colored troops. Upon discharge she moved to New Mexico, Pueblo, Colorado before settling in Trinidad, Colorado. Suffering from the complications of diabetes, Cathay Williams had several toes amputated and walked with a crutch. She identified the cause of the amputations being from frostbite suffered on winter marches while in the Army. Williams applied for medical disability from the military in 1890 and 1893 and was denied each time despite there being precedents for women receiving disability compensation from the Army.

Cathy Williams' medical disability denial forms.

The date of her death is uncertain; however, she passed in Trinidad, CO. As noted earlier, Louis S. Warren describes the burgeoning success of Buffalo Bill's Wild West "as a beneficiary of the practice in the late 1800s…where newspaper editors hit on the technique of manufacturing news rather than merely reporting it."[1] And in this regard, an interesting editorial was found in the *Pueblo Daily Chieftain* dated April 22, 1897, some 21 years after the commonly accepted version of events in the life of Cathay Williams. A transcription of this article follows on page 83. ❈

ENDNOTES
1. *Buffalo Bill's America: William Cody and the Wild West Show*, Louis S. Warren 2005, p 158.

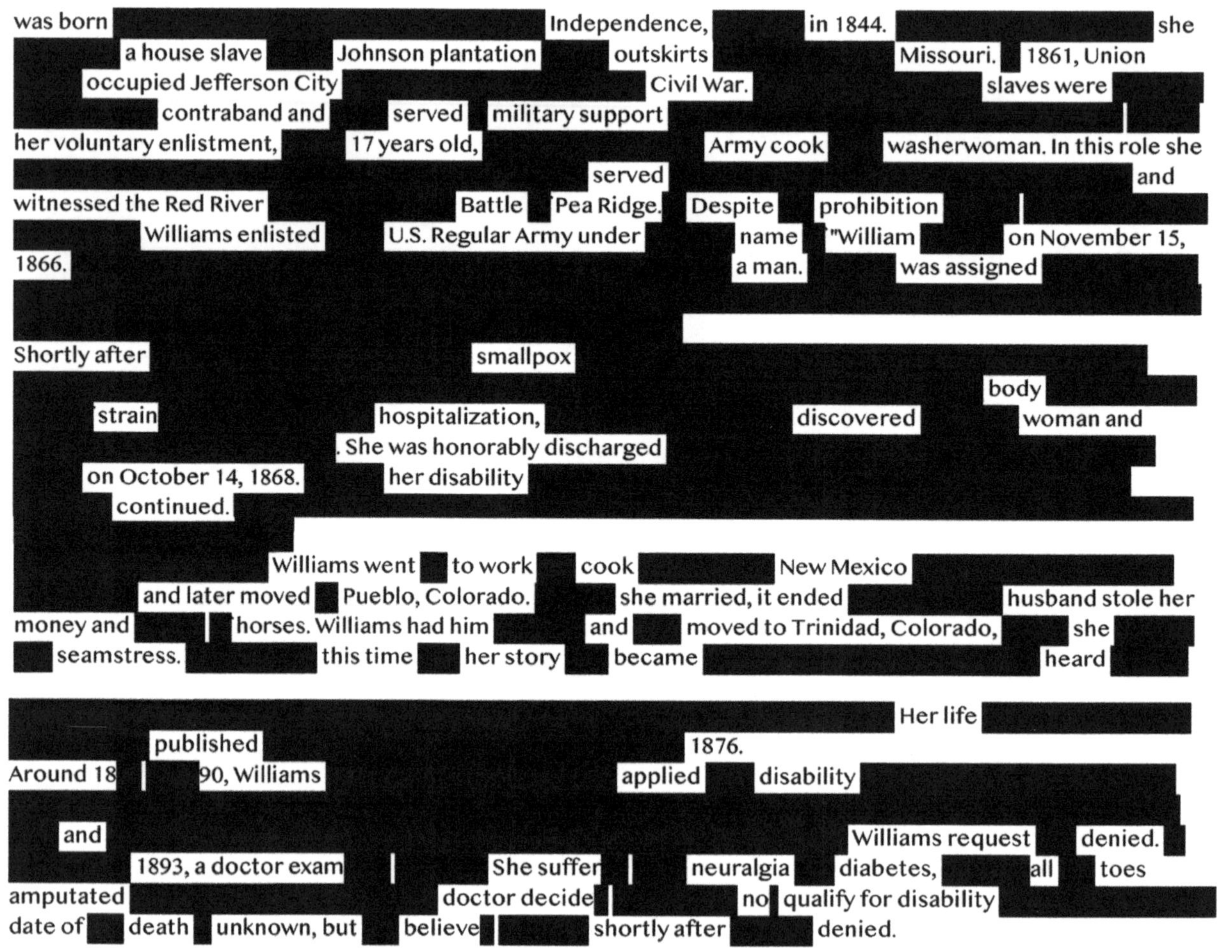

Mahogany L. Browne, *Cathay Williams blackout poem.*

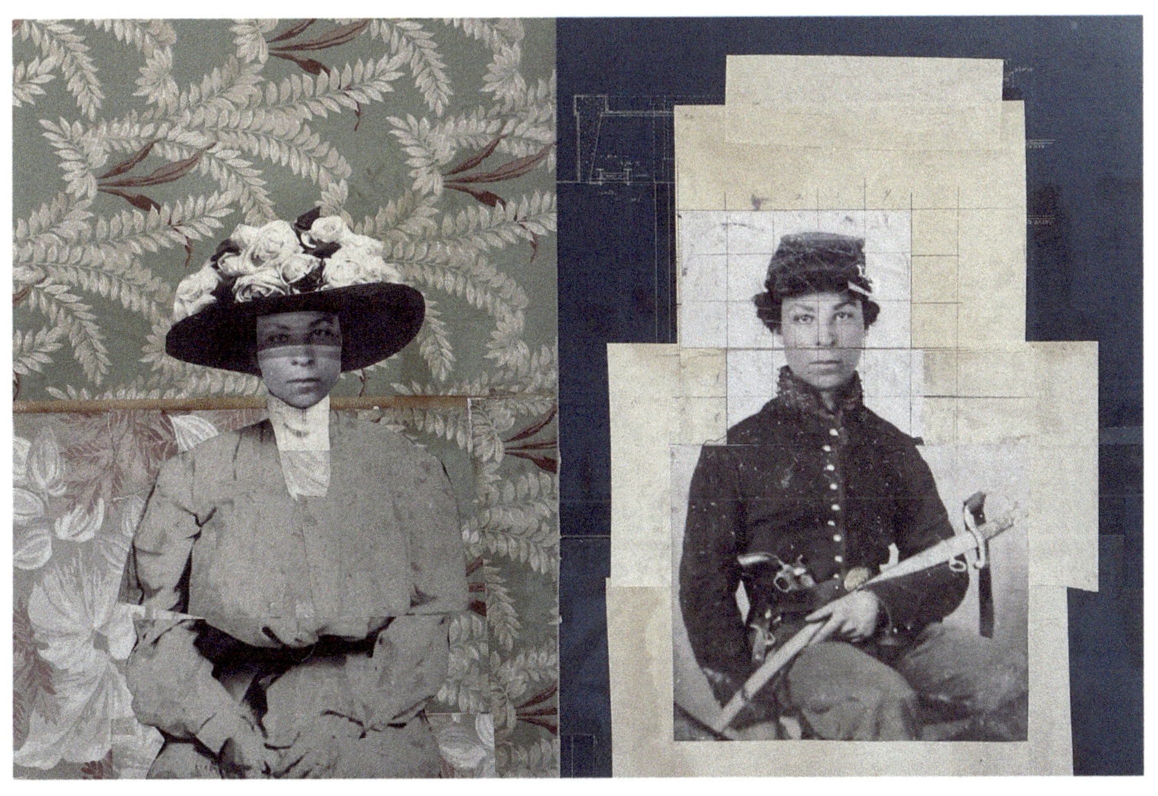

Tom Judd, *Two Cathays.*

CLAD AS A WOMAN FOR YEARS.

Negro Man who Worked as a Laundress in Pueblo.

COMMITTED TO THE ASYLUM.

Cathy Williams, Who Was Employed in Pueblo and Trinidad as Woman Servant, Turns Out to be a Man—Peculiar Case Brought to Light By Attack of Insanity.

Cathy Williams was a well known colored servant in Pueblo fifteen or twenty years ago and was employed as a laundress and nurse by many prominent families of the then young city. These people will be surprised to know that the faithful, respectful, modest woman was a man and is now an inmate of the insane asylum in this city, having ben sent here from the county court at Trinidad yesterday, suffering from a mild mania, his delusion being that an Italian with a bear is constantly following him and trying to force him to dance with the bear for the amusement of the public.

For twenty years or more this negro has successfully masqueraded as a woman without in any way giving rise to any suspicions as to his real sex. Except on the one subject of the bear and the Italian he is perfectly rational and is a splendid type of the deferential house servant of the ante-bellum days in the south. His only answer to a question as to why he took to wearing woman's clothes is that he just wanted to. No other reason is known. Telling of his life he says he served through the civil war and was a body servant of General Sherman and to General Grant also.

Soon after the close of the war and when he had begun to wear women's clothes, he came to Pueblo and worked in half a dozen prominent families whose names he mentions. Some few years ago he went to Trinidad and as a woman was employed as a nurse and laundress and was and still is as highly regarded by every one there as in Pueblo.

Five or six months ago he gave evidence of insanity as spoken of above. He, or she as he was then known, was adjudged insane by the county court and was ordered committed to the insane asylum as Cathy Williams. There being no room for women patients at the asylum Cathy Williams was brought to this city and put in the private asylum then in existence in the Mount Pleasant house on Tenderfoot hill.

The physician in charge granted a private interview to the new patient at the patient's request. Cathy Williams then announced that "she" was a man and that "her" name was William Cathay. On account of his mental malady it was decided inadvisable then to compel Cathay to change habits of dress that had existed for twenty years and accordingly he was allowed to continue to wear dresses, and was assigned quarters apart from the other patients. Though from his dress apparently a woman Cathay seemed to have had an intense antipathy for all women and avoided them as much as possible. He was put in charge of the laundry but said nothing to the other women except to issue his instructions and he ran the department to perfection.

Finally the peculiar conditions necessitated in the care for Cathay and the demand for room for other patients, several of whom could be provided for in the quarters assigned him, decided the management of the institution, which is now located in the L. B. U. property on Victoria avenue, to notify the Las Animas county authorities to remove Cathay. He was taken back to Trinidad Sunday attired as a woman and known officially as Cathy Williams. But Cathy Williams passed out of existence in the county court there Monday when William Cathay was adjudged insane. The individual who left Pueblo as a woman Sunday came back yesterday as William Cathay, a man, and was committed to the insane asylum where he now is.

Cathay was resplendent in new clothes when he reached the city yesterday and seemed to enjoy his changed dress and the freedom from the deception which he had maintained for so many years. He is about fifty years of age, moderately stout and of medium height. Some years ago he froze his feet and amputation of the toes was necessary so that he walks in rather a halting fashion with the aid of a stick.

NOTICE.

Pueblo city warrants, series "R," numbered 6960 to 7195 inclusive, and warrants marked special levee numbered 3292, 3293, 3294, 3301, and 3305, will be paid on presentation at city treasurer's office. Interest on same ceases, April 29th, 1897.

C. L. FUNK,
City Treasurer.

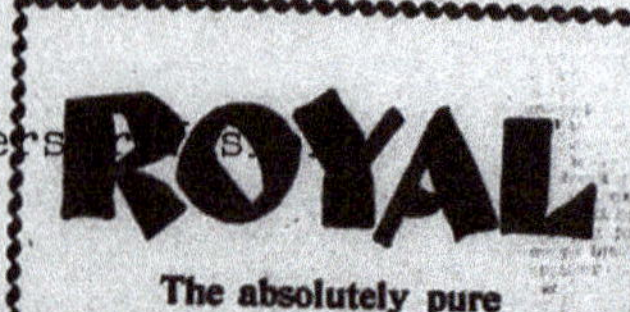

CLAD AS A WOMAN FOR YEARS
Negro Man who Worked as a Laundress in Pueblo Committed to the Asylum

Cathy Williams, Who Was Employed in Pueblo and Trinidad as a Woman Servant, Turns Out to be a Man—Peculiar Case Brought to Light by an Attack of Insanity.

Cathy Williams was a well-known colored servant in Pueblo fifteen or twenty years ago and was employed as a laundress and nurse by prominent families of the then young city. These people will be surprised to know that the faithful, respectful, modest woman was a man and is not an inmate of the insane asylum in this city, having been sent here from the county court at Trinidad yesterday suffering from a mild mania, his delusion being that an Italian with a bear is constantly following him and trying to force him to dance with the bear for the amusement of the public.

For twenty years or more this negro man has successfully masqueraded as a woman without in any way giving rise to any suspicions as to his real sex. Except on the one subject of the bear and the Italian he is perfectly rational and is a splendid type of the deferential house servant of the ante-bellum days in the south. His only answer to the question as to why he took to wearing woman's clothes is that he just wanted to. No other reason is known. Telling of his life he says he served through the civil war and was a body servant to General Sherman and to General Grant also.

Soon after the close of the war and when he had begun to wear women's clothes, he came to Pueblo and worked in half a dozen prominent families whose names he mentions. Some few years ago he went to Trinidad and as a woman was employed as a nurse and laundress and was and still is as highly regarded by everyone there as in Pueblo.

Five or six months ago he gave evidence of insanity as spoke above. He, or she as he was then known, was adjudged insane by the county court and was ordered committed to the insane asylum as Cathy Williams. There being no room for women patients at the asylum Cathy Williams was brought to this city and put in a private asylum then in existence in the Mount Pleasant house on Tenderfoot hill.

The physician in charge granted a private interview to the new patient at the patient's request.

Cathy Williams then announced that "she" was a man and that "her" name was William Cathay. On account of his mental malady, it was decided inadvisable then to compel Cathay to change habits of dress that had existed for twenty years and accordingly he was allowed to continue to wear dresses and was assigned quarters apart from the other patients. Though from his dress apparently a woman Cathay seemed to have had an intense antipathy for all women and avoided them as much as possible. He was put in charge of the laundry but said nothing to the other women except to issue his instructions and he ran the department to perfection.

Finally, the peculiar conditions necessitated in the care for Cathay and the demand for room for other patients, several of whom could be provided for in the quarters assigned him, decided the management of the institution, which is now located in the L. B. U. property on Victoria avenue, to notify the Las Animas county authorities to remove Cathay. He was taken back to Trinidad Sunday aired as a woman and known officially as Cathy Williams. But Cathy Williams passed out of existence in the county court there Monday when William Cathay was adjudged insane. The individual who left Pueblo as a woman Sunday came back yesterday as William Cathay, a man, and was committed to the insane asylum where he is now.

Cathay was resplendent in new clothes when he reached the city yesterday and seemed to enjoy his changed dress and the freedom from the deception which he had maintained for so many years. He is about fifty years of age, moderately stout and of medium height. Some years ago he froze his feet and amputation of the toes was necessary so that he walks in rather a halting fashion with the aid of a stick.

NOTE *There are no known surviving images of Cathay Williams.*

Born in 1844 on homelands of the Kansa and Osage peoples—six years before the Fugitive
Slave Act, four years after the Treaty of Guadalupe Hidalgo ended the Mexican American War,
fourteen years after the passage of the Indian Removal Act—

Born in the era aimed to civilize "merciless Indian savages" and Preserve slavery

Born at a Time when "any person who was not free would be counted as
three-fifths of a free individual"
When more than 100% was required from slave labor
(to work Indigenous [stolen] land)
When westward expansion excluded, extracted, wrestled with the
semantics of Emancipation
Of this soldier,
born in a township named Independence—answering the call for "men of African descent" to
"rally 'round the flag of freedom," to soldier "against hostile Indians"—duly "entitled to all
horses and other plunder taken from Indians"

Of this soldier, whose body and gender became an exercise in calculus, comparative studies in
American literature, a portrait of waywardness, consequential logic theorems at the purview of
white conforming scales

Of this soldier, freedom unfurls—released from the three-pronged iron collar dangling con-
scripted charms, released from the false-faced duties for colonial settler enjoyment, released
as object of parlor songs

dear Soldier—may you rest in your sweet land of liberty

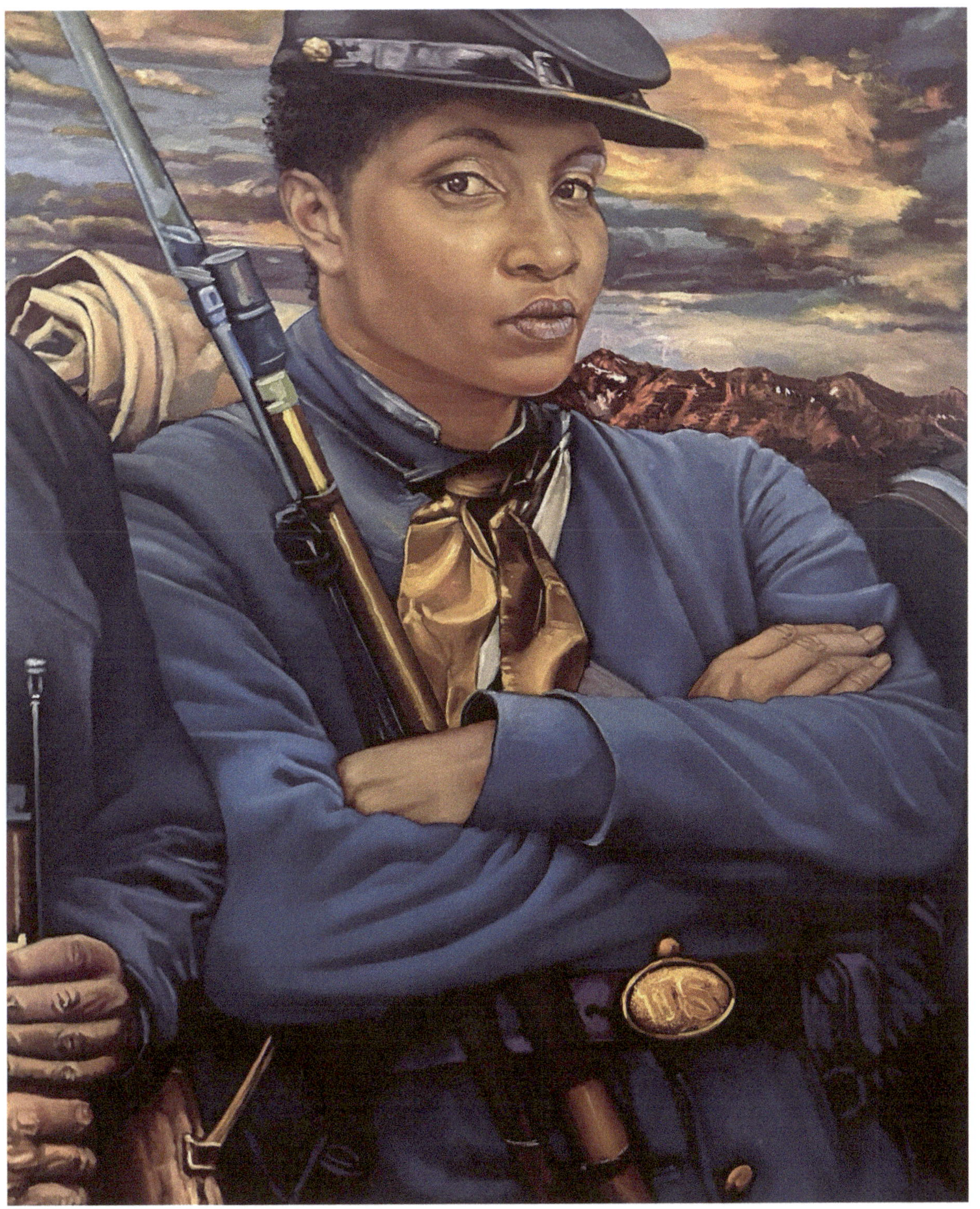

Gaia, *Cathay Williams*. Oil painting, 2023.

crimes against humanity

Chip Thomas

GEORGE WASHINGTON WILLIAMS WAS BORN A FREE MAN IN BEDFORD
Springs, Pennsylvania, in 1849. In 1864, "semiliterate, underage, and with an
assumed name, Williams enlisted in the 41st U.S. Colored Troops of the Union
Army."[1] Following the Civil War Williams continued his military career first in
Mexico where he was among Americans who joined the Army of the Republic
of Mexico under the command of General Espinosa, fighting to overthrow
Emperor Maximilian, brother-in-law to King Leopold II of Belgium. Upon com-
pleting this tour Williams reenlisted for a five-year stint in the U.S. Colored
Troops where he was assigned to the 10th Cavalry and participated in the Plains
Wars. Suffering a lung wound in 1868 Williams was discharged later that year
after recovery.

Once discharged Williams became in succession a Baptist minister, politi-
cian, lawyer, journalist and an historian who compiled a compendium of African American history titled *The History of the Negro Race in America 1619–1880*,
published in 1882. This expansive volume demonstrated the participation and
contributions of African Americans from the earliest days of the colony.

In the late 1880s, Williams learned of King Leopold II's independently-
owned colony in Central Africa called the Congo Free State (1885–1908). "Sick

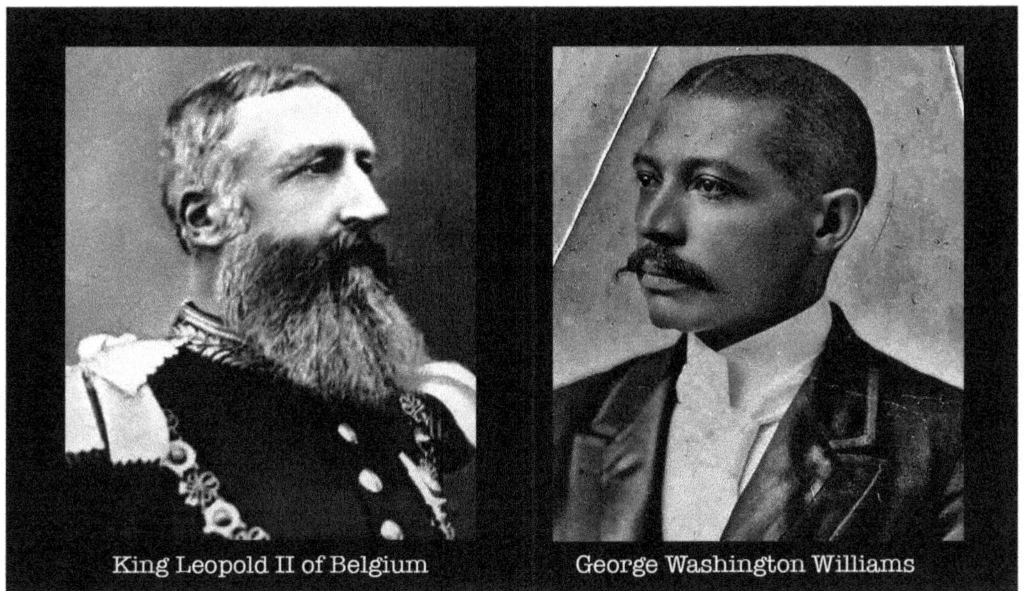

King Leopold II of Belgium   George Washington Williams

of the post-Civil War backlash of lynchings, Ku Klux Klan violence and the return of white supremacist rule throughout the South,"[2] Williams wanted to witness whether Leopold's private colony was the economic utopian paradise Leopold portrayed and journeyed there in 1890 at age 40.

Hochschild notes,

> Leopold's will treated the Congo as if it were just a piece of uninhabited real estate to be disposed of by its owner. In this the king was no different from other Europeans of his age, explorers, journalists, and empire-builders alike, who talked of Africa as if it were without Africans; an expanse of empty space waiting to be filled by the cities and railway lines constructed through the magic of European industry.
>
> To see Africa instead as a continent of coherent societies, each with its own culture and history, took a leap of empathy, a leap that few, if any, of the early European or American visitors to the Congo were able to make. To do so would have meant seeing Leopold's regime not as progress, not as civilization, but as a thief of land and freedom.[3]

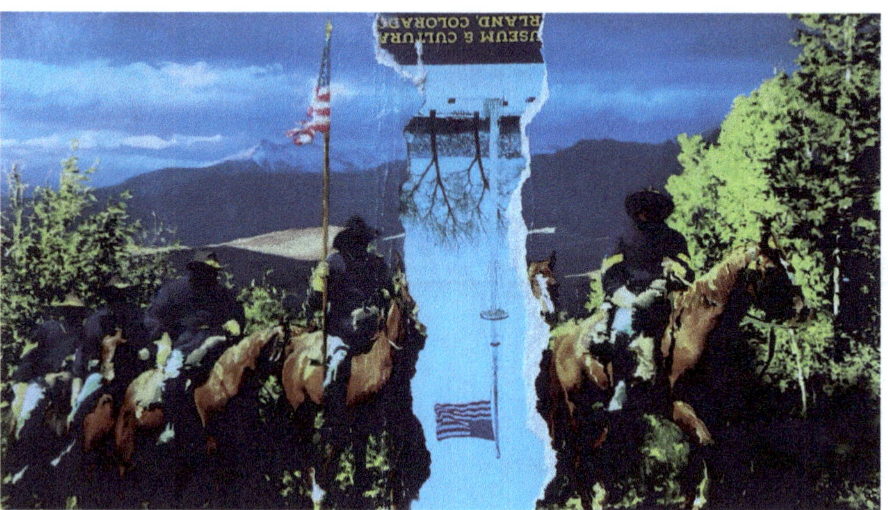

Fort Garland Museum & Cultural Cent
Fort Garland, Colorado

Today, visitors to Fort Garland (est. 1858) ca
explore life in a nineteenth military fort by wal
the parade grounds and touring five of the org
adobe buildings.

Before visiting the Congo Free State Williams lobbied the U.S. Congress in support of Leopold's desire for the U.S. to officially recognize the Congo Free State as a legitimate colony belonging solely to King Leopold.

Williams departed for the Congo Free State, despite Leopold's staunch objection, to learn if Leopold's colony was a safe and promising home for African Americans (whom southern whites were happy to get rid of.) Free blacks weren't getting 40 acres and a mule in the U.S.; perhaps they would in the Congo.

He left the Congo Free State appalled by the horrors he witnessed including forced labor camps to extract rubber, physical mutilation of workers who couldn't meet daily quotas and high rates of death. Williams penned a letter to Leopold titled "An Open Letter to His Serene Majesty Leopold II, King of the Belgians and Sovereign of the Independent State of Congo, by Colonel the Honorable Geo. W. Williams, of the United States of America" in which he detailed the atrocities witnessed and identified them as crimes against humanity. Williams was not a colonel, but it was his clarion call in 1890 that ignited the international abolitionist movement in Europe and the United States of which Mark Twain became involved.

Williams died penniless in Europe August 2, 1891, still advocating for his brothers in the Congo leaving one to wonder if Williams' participation in the Indian Wars sensitized him to identifying parallels with Leopold's regime such that he came to view Manifest Destiny "not as progress, not as civilization, but as a thief of land and freedom" as Hochschild suggests. ✸

buffalo soldiers: reVision

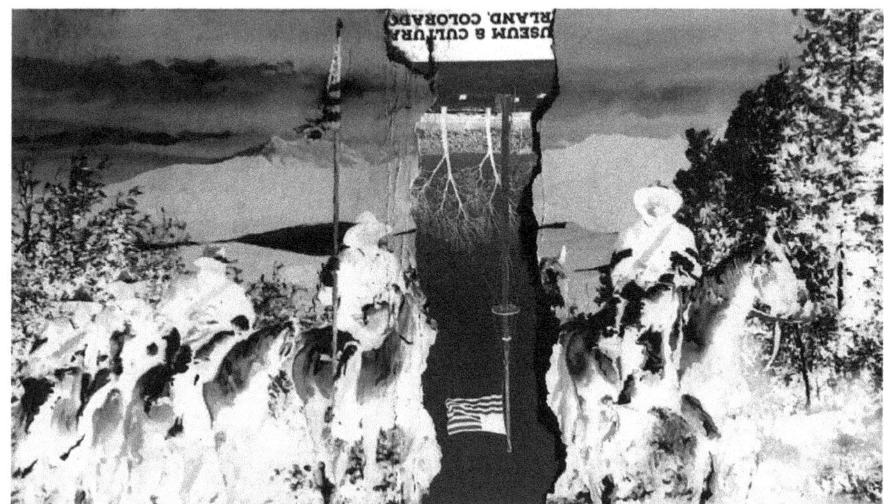

Theodore A. Harris, *For John Taylor and the Patriotic Syringe of Settler Colonialism*, collaged postcard printed on paper, triptych, 25"x44" each panel, 2023.

ENDNOTES
1. Adam Hochschild, *King Leopold's Ghost*. Houghton Mifflin, 1998. p 102.
2. Ibid. p 103.
3. Ibid. p 101.

living their best lives

contributors

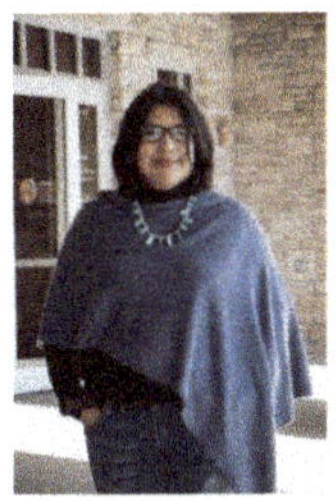

ESTHER G. BELIN is the author of two poetry books *From the Belly of My Beauty* (1999) and *Of Cartography* (2017), and co-editor of *The Diné Reader: An Anthology of Navajo Literature* (2022). She is a two-time recipient of the American Book Award from the Before Columbus Foundation. She is a graduate of the Institute of American Indian Arts and the University of California, Berkeley, and Antioch University, Los Angeles.

She is a citizen of the Navajo Nation and lives on the Colorado side of the four corners. She teaches in the Native American and Indigenous Studies department at Fort Lewis College, and the low-residency MFA in Creative Writing program at the Institute of American Indian Arts.

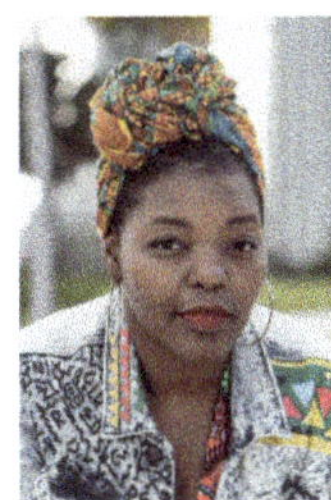

MAHOGANY L. BROWNE, selected as Kennedy Center's Next 50 and Wesleyan's 2022–2023 Distinguished Writer-in-Residence, the Executive Directory of JustMedia, Artistic Director of Urban Word, is a writer, playwright, organizer, and educator. Browne has received fellowships from All Arts, Arts for Justice, Air Serenbe, Baldwin for the Arts, Cave Canem, Poets House, Mellon Research, & Rauschenberg. She is the author of recent works: *Vinyl Moon, Chlorine Sky* (optioned for Steppenwolf Theater), *Woke: A Young Poets Call to Justice*, *Woke Baby*, and *Black Girl Magic*. Founder of the diverse lit initiative Work Baby Book Fair, Browne is currently touring her latest poetry collection *Chrome Valley* received a starred review from *Publisher's Weekly* and was highlighted in *The New York Times*.

She is the first-ever poet-in-residence at the Lincoln Center and lives in Brooklyn, NY.

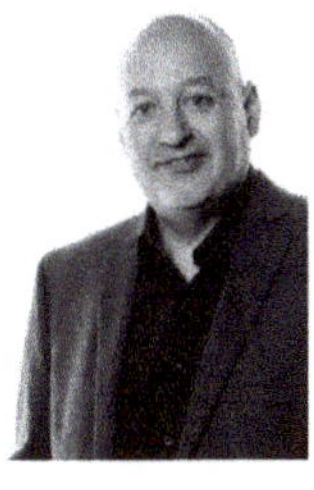

ERIC J. CARPIO is the Chief Community Museum Officer for History Colorado and the Director of the Fort Garland Museum & Cultural Center. At Fort Garland, he's leading the museum toward a renewed vision centered on co-creating and elevating diverse voices through community engagement and collaboration. Fort Garland's most recent exhibit, *Unsilenced: Indigenous Enslavement in*

Southern, has received extensive recognition by media outlets such as *The New York Times*, *Indian Country Today*, and Rocky Mountain PBS. In his role, Eric serves as the director of the Borderlands of Southern Colorado Educator Workshop, a National Endowment for the Humanities Landmarks of American History project, which explores the complex history of the American southwest through the intersection of racial, ethnic, religious, and geographic landscapes.

In 2019, he was selected as one of ten Senior Fellows for Diversity, Equity, Accessibility, and Inclusion (DEAI) for the American Association of Museums Facing Change initiative, to provide DEAI training, support, and leadership to museum boards across the country. Eric has a B.S. from Colorado State University and a M.A, from Adams State University. He is an alumnus of the University of Denver's Latino Leadership Institute (LLI) and the University of Pennsylvania's Center for Social Impact Strategy (CSIS).

ROSIE CARTER is a visual artist, writer and printmaker. She lives and works in the Four Corners region of southwestern Colorado where she explores its history and rugged rocky beauty in her everyday life and art. Working with screen printing, letterpress and mixed media, Carter investigates how the land and the humans who've lived here have influenced each other for millennia: the human igniting interludes of radiance and tragedy, the landscape holding it all in memory. Uncovering these memories and their genesis in history and geography is Carter's preoccupation, informing her art as well as efforts to understand the world.

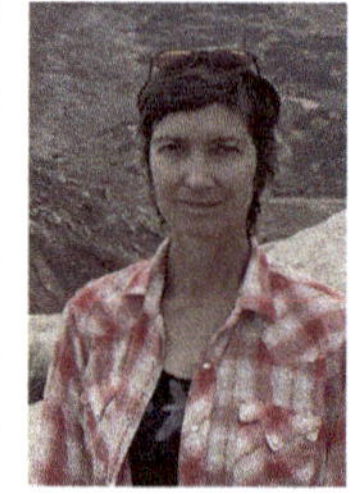

GAIA grew up in New York City and is a 2011 graduate of the Maryland Institute College of Art with a Bachelor in Fine Arts. His studio work, installations and gallery projects have been exhibited throughout the world most notably The Baltimore Museum of Art, Rice Gallery in Houston, the Palazzo Collicola Arti Visive in Spoleto and the Civil and Human Rights Museum in Atlanta. His street work has been documented and featured in several books on urban art, including *Beyond the Street: The 100 Leading Figures in Urban Art* (Berlin, 2010) and *Outdoor Gallery* (New York, 2014). Gaia was listed as a 2015 Forbes 30 Under 30 in Art and Style recipient in Art and Style and was a Fullbright beneficiary to study and paint in New Delhi and Bogotá on behalf of the State Department. In addition to a prolific and precocious artistic practice, Gaia has curated projects funded by the National Endowment for the arts, and consults

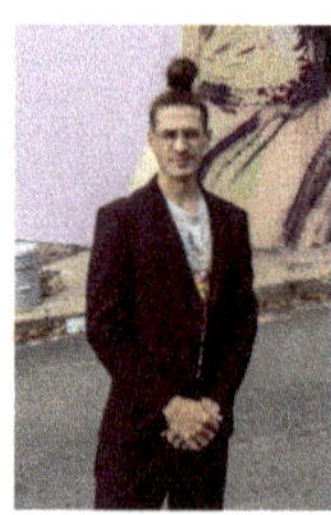

buffalo soldiers: reVision

with brands, organizations and government agencies on creative place-making projects. Gaia lives and works in Baltimore, Maryland, but spends a majority of his time painting murals across the world and has produced works in all six habitable continents.

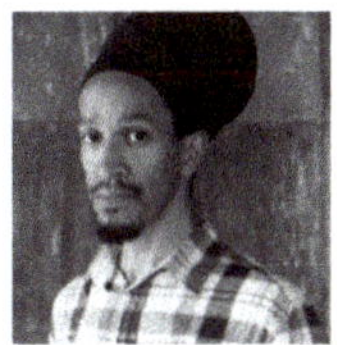

ANDRÉ LEON GRAY lives and works in his hometown of Raleigh, North Carolina as a self-trained multidisciplinary visual artist. Within his installations, tar paintings, drawings, collages, and assemblages, he explores and investigates power structures, social hierarchies, culture, and history. His artistic practice uses discarded and reclaimed objects charged with sociopolitical meaning to forge links between the past and the present to give the viewer a visual meal for the mind.

His exhibition and career highlights include: the Fountainhead Residency, Miami (2011); *African Continuum: International Year for People of African Descent*, United Nations Headquarters, New York (2011); *Dust My Broom: Southern Vernacular from the Permanent Collection*, California African American Museum, Los Angeles (2019-20); *To the Hoop: Basketball in Contemporary Art*, Weatherspoon Art Museum, University of North Carolina at Greensboro (2020); and *post hip hop? or return of the boom bap!*, Sikkema Jenkins & Co. Gallery, New York (2023).His artwork is in the permanent collection of the California African American Museum, North Carolina Museum of Art, and the Gregg Museum of Art & Design at NC State University.

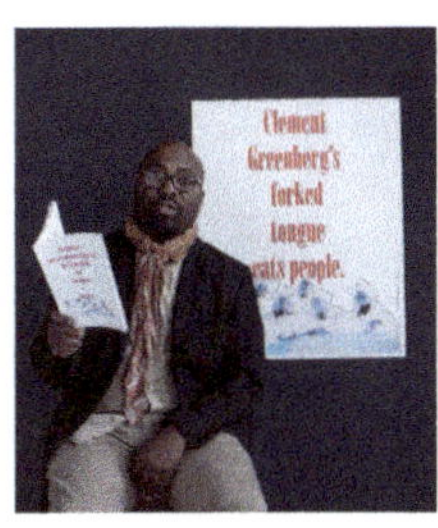

THEODORE A. HARRIS is a Philadelphia-based visual artist and poet. His work has been exhibited nationally and internationally and is in private and public collections such as University of New Mexico Art Museum, Saint Louis University Museum of Art, La Salle University Art Museum, Pennsylvania Academy of the Fine Arts, McGill University Visual Arts Collection, Center for Africana Studies; University of Pennsylvania, Kislak Center Rare Books and Manuscript Library; University of Pennsylvania, and the Petrucci Family Foundation Collection of African American Art, and the Winston and Carolyn Lowe Collection. Harris is the co-founder of the Anti-Graffiti Network/Philadelphia Mural Arts Program. Harris has also co-authored and authored books including *Our Flesh of Flames* (2019), *Malcolm X as Ideology* (2008) with Amiri Baraka, *TRIPTYCH* with Amiri Baraka and Jack Hirschman (2011), i ran from it and was *still* in it with Fred Moten (2007), and *Thesentür: Conscientious Objector to*

Formalism (2017). He is the Founding Artistic Director of The Institute for Advanced Study in Black Aesthetics. His recent exhibition *Theodore A. Harris: Art as Social Praxis Dedicated to Art Historian David Craven*, was mounted at Linfield University 2021 and was curated by Brian Winkenweder and Thea Gahr. He is a 2022 CFEVA Visual Artist Fellow (Center for Emerging Visual Artists).

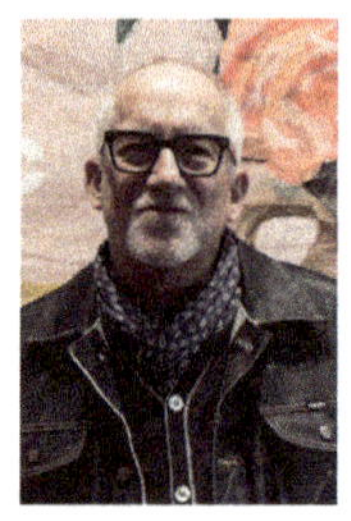

TOM JUDD's artistic journey began in Salt Lake City, where he spent his formative years before attending the prestigious Philadelphia College of Art. There, he studied with renowned artists such as Rafael Ferrer, Bob Kulicke, and Larry Day.

In 1979, Judd was included in a survey show entitled Contemporary Drawing: Philadelphia, curated by the esteemed Ann Percy and Frank Goodyear, at the Philadelphia Museum of Art. At the age of 25, Judd was among the featured artists, and his work was acquired by the museum for its permanent collection.

Judd went on to exhibit his work in distinguished galleries and museums throughout the country. His work has found its way into the collections of major institutions such as the Philadelphia Museum of Art, The Pennsylvania Academy of Art, and the Birmingham Museum of Art to name a few.

He presently works and lives in Philadelphia with artist wife Kiki Gaffney, and their daughter Astrid.

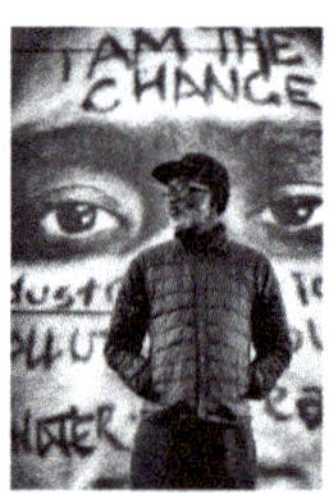

CHIP THOMAS, aka jetsonorama, is a photographer, public artist and physician who has been working in a small clinic on the Navajo Nation since 1987. There he coordinates the Painted Desert Project which he describes as a community building dialog which manifests as a constellation of murals painted by artists from the Navajo Nation as well as from around the world.

Thomas' own public artwork consists of enlarged black and white photographs pasted onto structures along the roadside primarily on the Navajo Nation. His motivation is to reflect to the community the love they've shared with him over the years. Thomas was a 2018 Kindle Project gift recipient and in 2020 he was one of a handful of artists chosen by the UN to recognize the 75th anniversary of the UN's founding. He has no formal artistic training but identifies strongly with the DIY energy of punk and hip hop.

resources

A Buffalo Soldier Speaks from National Park Service, October 14, 2020, https://www.nps.gov/yose/learn/historyculture/buffspodcast16-30.htm

Allen, James, Hilton Als, John Lewis, and Leon F. Litwack. *Without Sanctuary: Lynching Photography in America.* Twin Palms Publishers, 2000.

Atkinson, Rebecca. "Extraordinary Life along the Santa Fe Trail: Pueblo's Own Cathay Williams, Buffalo Soldier." Pueblo Archaeological and Historical Society Lecture, November 4, 2021, Pueblo, CO. https://www.youtube.com/watch?v=l5j1AOqaHHA

Beeton, Jared; Saenz, Charles N., and Waddell, Benjamin. *The Geology, Ecology, and Human History of the San Luis Valley.* University of Colorado, 2020.

Bond, Anne. "Buffalo Soldiers at Fort Garland." *Colorado Heritage*, Spring 1996, pp. 28–29.

Brooks, James, editor. *Confounding the Color Line: The Indian-Black Experience in North America.* University of Nebraska, 2002.

Brooks, James. "Confounding the Color Line: Indian-Black Relations in Historical and Anthropological Perspective." *American Indian Quarterly*, Winter-Spring 1998, pp. 125–133.

"Buffalo Soldiers." *The Stoop: Stories from across the Black Diaspora*, August 20, 2021, http://www.thestoop.org/home/2021/9/13/ep-52-buffalo-soldiers

Chang, David. *The Color of the Land: Race, Nation, and the Politics of Landownership in Oklahoma, 1832–1929.* University of North Carolina, 2010.

Delaney, Michelle. *Art and Advertising in Buffalo Bill's Wild West.* University of Oklahoma Press, 2019.

Gwaltney, William and Welle, Thomas. "By Force of Arms: The Buffalo Soldiers of Colorado." *Colorado Heritage*, Spring 1996, pp. 30–34.

Hochschild, Adam. *King Leopold's Ghost: A Story of Greed, Terror, and Heroism in Colonial Africa.* Houghton Mifflin, 1999.

Johnson, Shelton. *Gloryland.* Counterpoint, 2009.

Katz, William. *Black Indians: A Hidden Heritage.* Atheneum Books for Young Readers, 2012.

Kenner, Charles. *Buffalo Soldiers and Officers of the Ninth Cavalry 1867–1898*. University of Oklahoma, 1999.

Mays, Kyle. *An Afro-Indigenous History of the United States*. Beacon Press, 2021.

McAllister, Louis Gregory. *John Taylor and Racial Formation in the Ute Borderlands 1870–1935*. 2013. Northern Arizona University, Thesis.

McGue, D. B. "John Taylor: Slave Born Colorado Pioneer." *The Colorado Magazine*, September 1941, pp. 161–68.

Porter, Mary Jean. "Buffalo Gal." *The Pueblo Chieftain*, June 9, 2009.

"Press of the West." *Colorado Experience*. Rocky Mountain PBS. August 14, 2020. https://www.pbs.org/video/colorado -experience-press-of-the-west-2jmq53/

Quintana, Frances. *Ordeal of Change: The Southern Utes and Their Neighbors*. AltaMira Press, 2004.

"Ranger Shelton Johnson Speaks about African American History Month 2021." Yosemite National Park. February 10, 2021. https://www.youtube.com/watch ?v=-0B2-HF1AOo

Sawyer, Michael. "The Buffalo Soldiers and Service in Times of Injustice." Borderlands of Southern Colorado Online Lecture Series, August 14, 2020, History Colorado. Lecture. https://www.youtube.com/watch ?v=e2kNF2Nw-y4&list=PLl68fplNJM8 DloYD2a5Xum4ORsRSWKZGS&index=7

Schubert, Frank. *Voices of the Buffalo Soldiers: Records, Reports and Recollections of Military Life and Service in the West*. University of New Mexico, 2008.

Taylor, Quintard. "Comrades of Color: Buffalo Soldiers in the West: 1866-1917." *Colorado Heritage*, Spring 1996, pp. 3–27.

Taylor, Quintard. "Intersections between Native American and African American History in the West."

The Shifting Borders of Race and Identity: A Research and Teaching Workshop On the First Nations and African American Experience, February 23, 2004, University of Kansas. Presentation. http://www .shiftingborders.ku.edu/presentations /taylor.html

Warren, Louis. *Buffalo Bill's America: Bill Cody and the Wild West Show*. Knopf, 2005.

Williams, Nancy. *Buffalo Soldiers on the Colorado Frontier*. History Press, 2021.

"Women of the Santa Fe Trail." Colorado Experience. Rocky Mountain PBS. November 9, 2022. https://www.pbs.org /video/women-of-the-santa-fe-trail -okubmo/

"Yosemite: Ranger Shelton Johnson on the Buffalo Soldiers and Diversity in the National Parks." *Everybody's National Parks*, October 31, 2019, https://www.every bodysnationalparks.com/shelton-johnson -buffalo-soldiers-diveristy-in-national -parks

Dear Nettie,

I wish I were more competent to the task of giving words to the things I have seen. I am unable to describe the majesty of this land and grandeur of spectacle I have witnessed. Indians are a mighty brilliant spectacle. They fight with a freedom spirit that does not excite sympathy for their sufferings. Being perplexed to know that freedom, I felt so desolate and alone.

Being born and reared in Slavery has tempered my feelings about events I have undergone and people I have met. The life of a solider gives me not much leisure and I only have irregular intervals to write you.

Dear Nettie,

The land here is vast and deep. When I think I have seen majesty, I witness something more brilliant than before. I know why the Indians fight so hard to keep this way of nomadism. I long for that spirit as military duties snatch every moment to seek opportunities before me.

Dear Nettie,

I do earnestly desire to talk the Indian language. I want to gain a realizing sense of the condition they are suffering. Is it the sense of being in bondage? How deep and dark and foul is their pit of abominations? I fear that I and the Indian share that secrecy.

Dear Nettie,

May the blessing of God rest upon this imperfect effort to civilize the Indian. In my way, there is no container strong enough to hold a human spirit. I believe those who encounter Indians will not dispose to doubt their veracity.

Dear Nettie,

With trifling explanations are we given orders. Sometimes the monotony stifles. The reprieve is the majesty of the land, the clear, sharp glint of the sun opening the day, and closing into inky black skies with stars as bright as fireflies.

Dear Nettie,

I wonder if this correspondence will naturally excite you seeing that I was raised in Slavery without the ability to read or write. I cannot say I have frequent intercourse with intelligent military persons as the indecorum of some men is abhorrent, nevertheless stated to be in the interest of the Indian's welfare. The toilsome duties help appease the intellectual indifference.

Dear Charlotte,

The company unit live together in a barracks separate from others, and we work to shield a comfortable living but the winter snow and wind cut into any comfort we had, thus, we were desirous of wearing buffalo robes like the Indian. We laughed heartily at that idea!

Dear Charlotte,

There was an Anglo-Saxon church man who I am indebted for many comforts. In secrecy, I received portions of crackers, cakes, and preserves from time to time. I bless his memory as the latest outbreak of disease took his life.

Dear Charlotte,

Today I was assigned the disagreeable duty of escorting an Anglo-Saxon wife of a Lt. to the market. That blight unpleasant was not without murmuring. The wife was not kind nor cruel, and after a brief period of suspense, the duty ended in a cordial manner. How earnestly I prayed in my heart that I would not be remembered for my faithful service!

Dear Charlotte,

The Anglo-Saxon scant views the Indian as God-breathing machines, no more valuable than the wild game hunted, or the horses they tend.

My solace lies in the vastness of the skies. The deep silence from the dawning of day and the innumerable quantity of stars in the heavens at night.

Dear Charlotte,

Today we encountered, cold looks, cold treatment and cold words. What blasphemous doctrine for one born into Slavery to be desirous of freedom! My heart rebels at God! What number of things must be taken from me!

Dear Charlotte,

The Anglo-Saxon says "Take courage, Willie, brighter days will come by and by." What does the Anglo-Saxon know about desires of freedom? What does the Anglo-Saxon know about the turmoil immense as the blowing sand on the plains?

Dear Charlotte,

Laborious years have passed since I first witnessed bloodshed. The snap from hundreds of blows falling on a human being, the piteous groans. The sound of agony rings in my ears once more.

Though they lose direction, they shall seek
Though they submerge into nebulous depth,
They shall taste once more the sweetness of breath
Featherlike gales from the Great Mystery's canticles

Buttressed—adjacent to the claims—a beguiled parallelism
(enslaved) (not) (human) (not) = itemized cargo (not but claimed) commodity
line-item
                        -izing
                        reconciling
                                    quarterly
                                            reporting

How does the Great Mystery reconcile an intentional breach of creation?
Threading apart radio wave aberrations in anointed breath?
A repatriated tally sheet of those laid to rest by a smothered spirit
Last breath regurgitating mineraled mountain weepings, seeking

Instruments of the United States government—implements of record—recounting white
settler

Sentimentality as tomb stones

O this decree is to be enforced by all the Nation, the power of
Tis duty of every Government conscription, to thereof protect
Its citizens. This is our golden moment! Join in the Fight! Battles
Guaranteed to light Liberty on this the soil of our birth, and shackles

Those of African descent, proceed immediately to Ft. Garland
Colonial sabers slaughtering Indigenous brethren, hostiles
Under the same flag. From this day forward the rules governing
Buffalo soldiers, Anglo expansionism enslaving, shackling down
a Reconstruction-era dog fight, dog collar hold, pegged down deep.

O this decree is to be enforced by all the Nation, the power of
Those of African descent, proceed immediately to Ft. Garland
Guaranteed to light Liberty on this the soil of our birth, and shackles
a Reconstruction-era dog fight, dog collar hold, pegged down deep.

Colonial sabers slaughtering Indigenous brethren, hostiles
Tis duty of every Government conscription, to thereof protect
Under the same flag. From this day forward the rules governing
Its citizens. This is our golden moment! Join in the Fight! Battles
Against division of land and spirit, birthright and shackles.

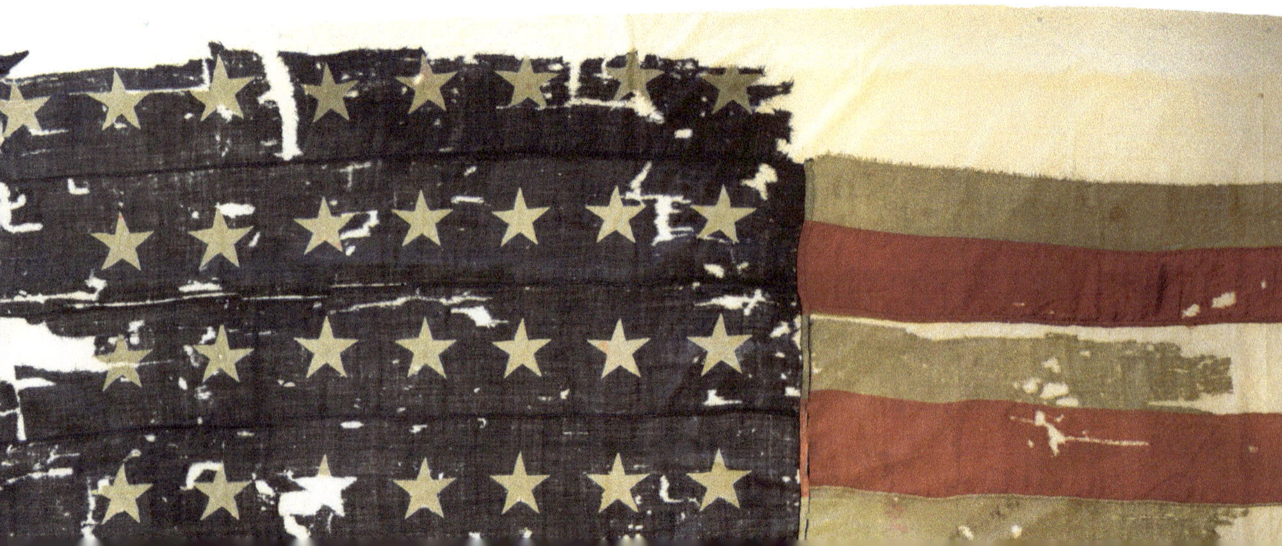

prayer for the flag

Senescent and Domicile
when I enter this Holy Ground
I acknowledge the Shadowed Ones
Those whose Freedoms
were Limited by this flag, who
carry alternating stripes on their
backs—To those tribes wiped out
to form the original 13 colonies

O how this land, this revered earth
hears Confession, wipes clean
vile altars, desecrated blood offerings
O how she responds, revolts in
torrents, tossing the surface dwellers
about—those who still do not heed
her groans

O how this people, this scattered people
bears Conscription, wets glean
magnifies shine, neatly enfolds regal
Anointing, fallow-fancy, settler-sown
O how the people contort majesty
glints of tarnished valor falsely wave
and of those unduly sacrificed—
May the 50 stars shine brightly

O how the dead, these dead among us
spew fricatives, the snap of linen in wind
the snap of bone underfoot the
tyrannical-seared boot
atomic half-lives, engineered invasion
each star, each stripe, a hand maiden's
rendering
O how the death unsettles into a unified
gait, my hip swings slowly 'round, footstep
pressing and pressing, smoothing down

I acknowledge the Holy Ground
when I enter this Shadowed place
Senescent and Domicile
I acknowledge the Blanca peak—whose
shadow braces memory to this land, and
those braceros who labored on this land
O Sisnaajiní, White Shell Mountain, your
shoulders extend the bloodlines deeper and
deeper into the core of where I stand